THE WORLD OF KEBABS

The World of KEBABS

Anand Prakash

whitecap

The information in this book is true and complete to the best of our knowledge. All
recommendations are made without guarantee on the part of the author or Whitecap
Books Ltd. The author and publisher disclaim any liability in connection with the use
of this information. For additional information, please contact Whitecap Books Ltd.,
351 Lynn Avenue, North Vancouver, British Columbia, Canada v7j 2c4.

Editor: Elaine Jones
Proofreader: Lesley Cameron
Design: R-house/Roberta Batchelor
Photography: Michael Tourigny
Food styling: Eric Akis

PRINTED IN CANADA BY FRIESENS

LIBRARY AND ARCHIVES CANADA CATALOGUING IN PUBLICATION
Prakash, Anand, 1932–
The world of kebabs/Anand Prakash.
Includes index.
ISBN 1-55285-789-1
ISBN 978-1-55285-789-2
1. Skewer cookery. I. Title.
TX834.A53 2006   641.7´6   C2005-906775-6

The publisher acknowledges the support of the Canada Council and the Cultural
Services Branch of the Government of British Columbia in making this publication
possible. We acknowledge the financial support of the Government of Canada through
the Book Publishing Industry Development Program for our publishing activities.

For information on other titles by Whitecap Books,
please visit our website at www.whitecap.ca.

Contents

ACKNOWLEDGMENTS

The idea of writing a book on kebabs of the world germinated some 25 years ago, and since then I have been researching and compiling information from around the world. During this period, I must have met hundreds of people from all walks of life in different countries who, one way or another, directly or indirectly, helped in my task of collecting material for this book. With the passage of time, it is almost impossible to recollect their names, let alone faces, but I do wish to acknowledge their help which enabled me to embark on this project.

There are several people, however, whose interest and assistance in the completion of this book have been generous and inspiring and I would like to specifically thank the following for their valuable advice.

Eric Akis, Canadian food columnist and author of several cookbooks, provided guidance on design, publication and illustrations; Michael Tourigny assisted in colour photography; my friend Benedict Ho, who first introduced me to the art of making satays; Sabiha Begum, food consultant to the Regency College of Hotel Management and Catering Technology and its chef Vishwa Nath Pande in Hyderabad, India, for arranging a demonstration of the most elaborate kebabs that I have ever seen. K.M. Srinevas and Mohammed Ikhlakh Quraishi, chefs at the Great Kebab Factory Restaurant at the Radisson Hotel in New Delhi; and chefs and staff at Karim Hotel in old Delhi who introduced me to a whole array of Indian kebabs and their history. Naga and Bernie Ampalam of Kuala Lumpur and Jasmin Abdullah Sahib of Singapore triggered my culinary curiosity for Malaysian and other Southeast Asian satays. Miyuki Mukogawa of Fukui City in Japan introduced me to a whole variety of yakitori preparations. Chefs and staff at Afanti Restaurant in Beijing, China; Onbasilar Kebap House in Istanbul, Turkey; and Persopolis Iranian Restaurant in North Vancouver, Canada, invited me into their kitchens to observe and record various kebab preparations and I am grateful for this courtesy. Others who helped me in many different ways include Richard and Jean Addison, Sheila Bhatnagar, Adam Holbrook, William and Beryl Neddow, Carol Lalli and Richard Veerapen. I am grateful for their assistance.

Lastly, and most important of all, I owe a debt of gratitude to my wife, Nancy McDuffe, who was the guinea pig during my experimenting with kebabs. She was responsible for, as she puts it, "quality and taste control" and I relied upon and respected her judgment. One day, in utter exasperation, she said, "Please stop, your kebabs are coming out of my ears!" That is when I started writing this book.

INTRODUCTION

ABOB, KABAB, KABAUB, KEBOB, KEBAP, KEBAB, SHISH KEBAB, SHASHLYK, SHISHLIK, SZASZLYKI, SOUVLAKI, BROCHETTE, PINCHOS, SPIEDINI, ESPETADA, SATAY, SATE, SATEH, SUYA, YAKITORI— NO MATTER WHAT NAME YOU CALL THEM OR HOW YOU SPELL IT, THESE PIECES OF MEAT, POULTRY, FISH OR SHELLFISH, STRUNG TOGETHER ON SKEWERS AND GRILLED TO PERFECTION ON AN OPEN FIRE, ARE TANTALIZING BITES.

Kebabs are eaten around the world, and in several countries they are a common street or fast food. Their popularity is well deserved: they have eye appeal and a delectable taste, their wonderful aroma of grilled meat and fat permeates the air, and they are a relatively inexpensive treat. Not only that, the relaxed outdoor cooking style provides a wonderful opportunity for socializing and enjoying food with family and friends.

Meat and various vegetables are threaded onto a skewer to produce an attractive and colorful presentation of food. Not only are they easy and fast to cook, they are also quite versatile and work as appetizers or main dishes. Because the meat pieces used in kebab cookery are cut into small cubes or thin strips and tenderized by marinating, it is acceptable to use less tender, inexpensive cuts of meat.

With an increasing emphasis on low-fat foods and less meat and more vegetables in the diet, skewer cooking seems well suited to today's casual culinary lifestyle. Kebabs offer a healthy alternative to grilling large slabs of meat—a 10–12 oz (280–340 g) steak, cut into shish kebab-size pieces can easily feed two people instead of one when the meat is threaded onto skewers with vegetables. Not only can a skewer hold all the major food groups, it is also possible to use any combination of meats, marinades, vegetables, seafood and even fruits. Kebabs can be prepared in advance and cooked at the last minute when your guests arrive. Kebab cooking can also be made inclusive and more fun by inviting your guests to assemble and grill their own kebabs as they please.

This book is the result of my longstanding interest in international cooking, extensive international travels and endless experimenting with old and new recipes collected from various countries. It may seem unusual for a marine biologist and an environmental scientist who has spent most of his professional life writing scientific research publications to write a cookbook devoted exclusively to kebabs of the world. Furthermore, I grew up in a strictly vegetarian family and was not introduced to any kind of meat until I left home at age 20 to attend universities in India and Canada. My love of travel and subsequent professional involvement in research and consulting with various government and international organizations provided me with ample opportunities to visit exotic destinations around the globe and to sample regional cuisines.

My interest in kebab cookery began in 1980 in Puerto Rico when I was visiting the University of Puerto Rico in Mayaguez. After a rather hectic day, I returned to my hotel late in the evening, wondering where to go for dinner that night. I stepped onto the balcony facing a city park and experienced the tantalizing aroma of grilled barbecued meat coming from nearby. I literally followed my nose and found myself standing near a hand cart parked near the park and equipped with a large charcoal brazier over which skewers of marinated pork were being grilled. The vendor was basting the meat with a spiced sauce and occasionally threw spoonfuls of fat on the burning coals. The smoke this generated attracted hungry customers. Once the kebab pieces were cooked, he brushed some butter on a split long bread and served the grilled meat on it with a liberal squirt of barbecue sauce. It was one of the tastiest and most satisfying street foods I had ever had, and it went down quite well with an ice-cold Puerto Rican beer on that sultry evening in Mayaguez.

That experience, some 25 years ago, prompted my quest to explore the world of kebabs. However, I did not make much progress because I discovered that raising my family and developing a professional career were full-time commitments that did not permit the luxury of traveling to faraway places, espe-cially with my own limited financial resources at that time. My subsequent travels through Europe, the Middle East, Asia, Africa, North and South America, the Caribbean, Australia, New Zealand, Hawaii and a few Pacific Islands convinced me that, although regional cuisines are a product of geography, climate, demography and availability of indigenous cooking ingredients, the art of cooking small pieces of meat, fish or poultry threaded onto a skewer and grilled over an open fire is truly international.

I found succulent kebabs in places as diverse as Djemaa el-Fna square in Marrakech, Morocco; the Estadio Nacional (football stadium) in Lima, Peru; the Satay Club and hawker centers in Singapore; street vendors in the alleys and lanes of Bangkok, Jakarta and Kuala Lumpur; food stalls outside Jama Masjid Mosque in Delhi and Tank Bundh in Hyderabad, India; Yakitori bars in Tokyo and other Japanese cities, and open-air stalls or kebab houses throughout the Mediterranean and Middle Eastern countries. In fact, in most of the countries, grilled kebabs were still a common street food and popular inexpensive snack, despite the recent invasion by numerous Western-style fast-food outlets.

Although the idea of writing a book on kebabs germinated in the early 90s soon after my retirement, it took another 10 years to seriously begin the project. I must confess to a lack of sustained effort on my part in researching, compiling and writing down the extensive material on kebabs of the world; it seemed such a daunting task. I felt that there was never enough geographical coverage, never enough authentic recipes and never enough personal observations to make this book a comprehensive treatise on kebabs of the world. So there was a compelling need for more travel to exotic destinations, meeting with people in the kebab trade—from modest street vendors to celebrated chefs—compiling new and authentic recipes, testing, tasting and refining cooking techniques that can be easily adapted at home.

Then in 1998 my wife, Nancy, presented me with a birthday gift, a book entitled *Barbeque Bible* by Steven Raichlen—a truly fascinating account of his travels to over 25 countries during a period of three years to research and observe barbecuing and grilling practices. The author has done a superb job and his book helped me in several ways. First, it reinforced my observations on kebab cookery from the early 80s in South America, Caribbean and the Orient; second, it guided me to concentrate on those countries where my information was incomplete or lacking; and finally, it provided me with an impetus to get on with the job of writing and completing this book.

This book was never meant to be simply a compilation of kebab recipes from around the world. I wanted to take a holistic look at kebab culture and explore how it became established, flourished and migrated to other geographical regions. Since there are countless kebab recipes characteristic of a particular geographic region, I have included here only the most popular ones available to the general public in each country. I have tried to stay away from exotic recipes concocted by master chefs in classy dining establishments and given fancy names. My sources for recipes have been street-food vendors, restaurant owners, chefs, food writers, food critics, libraries and the Internet. As someone who became interested in international cooking but never claimed more than marginal cooking expertise, I enjoyed not only soliciting recipes and advice from anyone who was willing to oblige, but also trying out and experimenting with various recipes at home.

Most of the recipes collected from over 60 countries have been tested and retested in our kitchens, some improvised without sacrificing their indigenous characteristic for simplicity and wider acceptance. In order to present each recipe in an orderly, concise and easily readable style, a standard recipe format was developed that identifies the recipe by its English name and also its country of origin and local name. Although the term "kebab" is used in some countries for meat preparations that may not be grilled and cooked without being threaded onto a skewer, for the purpose of this book, kebabs refer only to pieces of meat, poultry, fish, shellfish and vegetables that are cooked with the help of metal, wooden or bamboo skewers.

By and large I found no difficulty in exchanging information about recipes when talking to street vendors and small restaurant owners and chefs. Getting precise information from master chefs in well-established restaurants and eateries proved difficult, however, as they were generally reticent about sharing their favorite recipes. A few years ago I had the pleasure of meeting India's King of Kebab, Haji Mohammed Raees, fondly known as "Bade Mian," at his famous kebab house near Akbari Mosque in the North Indian city of Lucknow. Despite his fame, the master kebab maker was a simple unassuming and gracious old man who politely refused to divulge any details of his recipes which he treasures as his family secret. It now seems that his sons are carrying on the family tradition of kebab cookery in a well-known restaurant in New Delhi. Most of the master chefs in India and elsewhere work in the same way: recipes are memorized, jealously guarded, never publicly recorded but handed down from generation to generation. Commercial considerations override the need to share one's culinary talent with the public at large, but the proprietary nature of cooking techniques and recipes makes it difficult for those who are trying to compile unambiguous authentic and indigenous recipes.

The culinary characteristics and traits of a region are a product of its geography, history, climate, culture, religion, indigenous fauna and flora and the availability of food ingredients. Recipes are not a static entity but are in a state of constant evolution; they are developed, modified, discarded or improved according to prevailing circumstances. The new generation of young cooks and chefs who have gone through formal training in established culinary institutions seem to have no reservations about sharing their knowledge and are eager to share their talent with the public. This is quite evident from the increasing popularity of TV cooking shows and the proliferation of cookbooks and cooking magazines. Furthermore, the Internet, with hundreds of websites devoted to food, provides access to a mind-boggling number of recipes and finding cooking information from around the world has never been so easy. All of this has expanded the culinary horizon beyond imagination for food lovers. I am optimistic that my modest contribution to the ever-expanding world culinary scene is worth the effort.

Historical and Geographical Perspective

FOOD HISTORIANS GENERALLY ATTRIBUTE THE origin of kebabs to ancient Turkey. From here the art of threading small pieces of meat onto skewers and grilling over an open fire traveled to neighboring Greece and the Balkans, and across the Mediterranean to North Africa and the Middle East. However, it now seems that, before the spread of Turkish influence, meat was already being cooked on skewers somewhere in the Caucasus—a mountainous region between the Caspian Sea in the east and the Black Sea in the west. This region is described as

a veritable Babel of languages, ethnic groups, territorial claims and never-ending conflicts. Although the modern Caucasus comprises only four independent nations—Russia, Georgia, Armenia and Azerbaijan, it is still regarded as one of the most linguistically and culturally diverse places on earth. Throughout its history the Caucasus has been under the influence of Greeks, Romans, Persians, Byzantines, Mongols, Arabs, Turks and Russians; all have left their mark on the customs and cuisines of this region. It is indeed an irony that, despite the intense linguistic and cultural diversity in the Caucasus, the popularity of kebab cookery among its inhabitants is a common unifying feature.

Being on the trade route between Europe and Asia, for centuries the Caucasus has seen many battles by rival groups. It is widely believed that both the soldiers of the Ottoman Turk armies and wandering nomads killed wild animals and cooked the meat on their swords and lances over an open fire. During its height (1453–1650) the Ottoman Empire extended into Eastern Europe, the Middle East and Inner Asia, and Turkish influence on the cuisine of these regions endures. As wild game was replaced by domesticated lamb, beef, pork and poultry, and the sword was replaced by smaller metal skewers, the art of grilling skewered meat over wood embers or charcoal fire spread all through Eastern Europe, the Mediterranean and the Middle East.

Another major culinary influence, particularly on the spread of kebab culture in the Middle East and Central and South Asia, has been that of Persia (modern Iran). The ancient Persian Empire was founded around 550 BC and extended from India to Egypt and included parts of Turkey and Greece. Rich and sophisticated Persian culture and cuisine flourished throughout the Empire and although later conquests by Greeks, Arabs, Turks and Mongols caused the Persian influence to dwindle considerably, its culinary influence lingered on. The Arabs, who ruled Persia until 1050, introduced Islam, Arabic script and Islamic culture in that region but failed to dislodge the superior Persian cuisine. Although geographically and politically recognized as a part of the Middle East, Iran today has much stronger culinary affinities with the Central and South Asian countries than with the Middle Eastern countries.

Throughout its history, kebab cookery has been associated with the Islamic world; it has thrived in predominantly Muslim countries and has continued to spread to other parts of the world where Muslim influence has been significant. It is believed that, in the eighth century, when the Iberian Peninsula of Spain came under Arab and Berber rule, the Persian-dominated cuisine of medieval Islam including lamb kebabs, flourished in the court kitchens of Cordoba and Grenada. Through subsequent Spanish conquests in the New World, the Islamic-influenced Spanish cuisine is said to have permeated the Americas and likely introduced kebabs in that region. Arab and Indian Muslim spice traders introduced grilled skewered meat in Java, Indonesia, spawning a satay culture that evolved and flourished under the Muslim inhabitants of Indonesia and Malaysia and later on spread to other South East Asian countries. In East Asia, kebab cookery is exclusively the domain of an ethnic Muslim minority, the Uighurs of Xinjiang region in western China. In Japan and Korea there is no established link between skewered meat grilling and Muslim influence but it is quite possible that other foreign influences may have been at play in this region. In the 16th century, the Portuguese were among the first Westerners to establish trade links with Japan. Some decided to settle there and influenced Japanese cuisine by introducing fried foods, such as tempura. The Portuguese were followed by the Dutch, who may have introduced skewered grilling to Japan through their colonial ties to Indonesia and their culinary experience with satays.

Although one might be tempted to compartmentalize a particular national cuisine as Chinese, Japanese, Indian, French, Italian and so on, a cuisine is never entirely national. It varies from place to place within the recognized boundaries of a particular country and evolves under cultural, religious, historical, climatic and demographic influences in the entire region. Most cookbooks deal with ethnic foods within the confines of national or geographical boundaries and not so much in the greater regional and cultural context. I have tried to approach the subject of kebab cookery from the point of view of cultural and culinary characteristics and affinities as they have developed over the entire region rather than on the basis of current geographical and political boundaries. Accordingly, this book is divided into nine regions that present distinct cultural and culinary characteristics as far as kebab cookery is concerned. These regions are Europe, the Middle East, Africa, Central and South Asia, Southeast Asia, East Asia, Latin America and the Caribbean, North America and Oceania.

Although non-Arabic countries like Iran and Afghanistan are often recognized as a part of the Middle East, they have much stronger cultural and culinary affinities with the Central and South Asian countries and therefore have not been included in that chapter. Likewise, the North African countries of Morocco, Algeria, Tunisia and Libya, traditionally recognized as Middle Eastern, have been excluded from that region because their culinary characteristics and affinities are more Mediterranean than Middle Eastern, thanks not only to Arabic and Turkish but also Spanish, French and Italian culinary influences. Newly independent countries of the Caucasus—Georgia, Armenia and Azerbaijan, which were a part of the Soviet Union until its collapse in

1991, are located in southwest Asia and influenced by the culinary cultures of Russia, Turkey and Iran, have not been grouped either with the Middle Eastern or the Central Asian Region. Their history, culture, language and religion place them closer to Eastern Europe than to the Middle East or Asia. Mexico, which is a North American country, is included with the Latin American group of countries because it has closer cultural and culinary affinities with Latin America than with the United States or Canada.

About Grilling

ONCE CONSIDERED A SUMMER ACTIVITY, GRILLing has become a year-round way to cook, particularly in North America, thanks to the popularity of charcoal and gas grills. Kebabs are usually cooked by direct grilling over an open fire. High heat, provided by glowing charcoal, wood or gas-heated lava rocks and tiles, sears the surface of the food, thus sealing in the juices while imparting a wonderful smoky flavor. Usually kebabs are cooked without any grill cover, but where a smoky flavor is important, covering the grill for a short time is quite acceptable. Although kebab grilling is easy, it demands constant attention because the cooking time is short. Do not place the food on the hot grill and walk away to do something else unless you want your kebabs overcooked or charred.

While a wide variety of grills are now available, kebab cookery does not require elaborate or expensive grilling equipment. In fact, in most countries where kebabs are popular, grilling is done on a simple metal firebox which may or may not be covered by a metal grate or grid. Simple portable charcoal grills like Japanese hibachis are ideal for grilling the small cuts of meat used in kebabs, satays and yakitori for a small crowd at a picnic. For larger gatherings, charcoal-burning brazier grills, kettle grills or gas grills are the answer.

There is no right or wrong choice when it comes to grills. Choose yours according to the number of people you are cooking for. Also remember to take into account your fuel preference: wood, charcoal or charcoal derivatives, gas or electricity. Grilling imparts a unique taste to foods that is not duplicated by other methods of cooking, no matter what type of grill you use.

Electric Grills

THESE ARE SIMPLE TO USE AND ELIMINATE fussing with messy charcoal and refilling of gas tanks. However, they do not generate a high enough heat to produce the characteristic smoky flavor of kebabs grilled over charcoal or gas. Although some grills have space to add wood chips to give a smoky flavor to the food, this artificial flavoring is not suitable for kebabs. For these reasons, electric grills are not recommended for serious kebab cooking.

Charcoal Grills

CHARCOAL GRILLS COME IN DIFFERENT SIZES and shapes, from simple open braziers to larger models equipped with an adjustable cooking grid and lid; more elaborate covered kettle grills have vents to control air flow and heat and can be used as an oven, smoker or grill. Every summer new charcoal models with gleaming stainless steel equipped with numerous accessories are displayed at hardware stores and supermarkets. Die-hard purists and kebab aficionados favor grilling over charcoal, which they claim imparts a unique flavor, although most people cannot tell the difference between kebabs cooked on a charcoal or a gas grill. Charcoal arguably remains the most popular fuel for grilling kebabs throughout the world, but the increasing popularity of gas grills, particularly in North America, has added a new dimension to kebab cookery.

Charcoal grills burn natural lump charcoal, hardwood or charcoal briquettes and are cheap, fairly portable and efficient. They also operate in most developing countries, where charcoal is readily available and is inexpensive. In the urban centers of Europe and North America, charcoal and charcoal products tend to be expensive in the long term. Some disadvantages include the need to store the fuel in a dry place; handling and disposing of the burnt ashes, which can be quite messy; and the need for an igniter that in some cases is a flammable substance transferring undesirable flavors to cooked food if not fully combusted. Lump wood charcoal made of softwood is easier to ignite but burns up quickly, thereby providing a limited window for proper cooking. Hardwoods such as oak, cherry, mesquite, maple, hickory, beech, birch and ash burn slowly and add a pleasant aroma to the grilled food, but first they need to be transformed into coals by smoldering under low oxygen conditions. The charcoal then requires constant attention to provide adequate and even heat during grilling. The coals are ready for grilling when a light coat of gray ash covers the surface and all the residue from the fire starters are burned off. Charcoal and charcoal briquettes are slow to heat and may take as long as 30 to 45 minutes to reach the ash stage suitable for grilling. Lack of proper heat control and a limited window of cooking time at optimum temperatures are the other disadvantages of charcoal grills.

Gas Grills

PROPANE- OR NATURAL GAS-FIRED GRILLS ARE equipped with lava rocks, ceramic tiles or metal flavorizer bars that, when heated, generate sufficient smoke as fat and meat juices drip on them to flavor cooked foods. Gas grills are more expensive to buy but are relatively inexpensive to operate in the long term. They are convenient, quick to light and provide instant heat; the cooking temperature can be controlled, giving a more or less uniform temperature throughout the cooking process; and they are easy to clean after use. Newer models come with side burners, electric rotisserie, heat sensors, temperature probe and a whole range of accessories. Portable gas grills use butane as their fuel source and are quite handy for campsite cooking but not necessarily for kebab grilling. I have used both charcoal and gas grills extensively to cook kebabs and have found little or no difference in taste. Gas grills are my personal preference.

Grilling Technique

KEBABS CAN BE COOKED DIRECTLY OVER A charcoal fire without a cover since charcoal burns hot; with gas grills, it may be necessary to put the lid down to create the high heat required for grilling the perfect kebab. Always bring kebabs to room temperature before grilling—this helps the meat cook more evenly and reduces the cooking time.

If the grill is equipped with a metal grate or grid, brush it with vegetable oil or use oil spray before preheating to prevent food from sticking. To prevent flare-ups do not oil or spray the grid after lighting the fire. The grilling grate should be kept clean by scrubbing with a stiff metal or nylon brush; there is nothing less appetizing than grilling kebabs on a grill grate already coated with bits of food from a previous meal. While grilling meat, fat and meat juices drip down on the hot charcoal, briquettes or heating element and produce flare-ups which may cause the meat to be overcooked or become coated with ash or black soot. To reduce flare-ups, remove excess fat from meat and baste sparingly with oil during cooking. A few squirts from a water spray bottle can effectively deal with flare-ups in charcoal grills; with gas grills, use the cover to briefly shut out the air supply.

For grilling kebabs on direct heat, cooking temperatures ranging from medium (350°F or 180°C) to high (500°F or 260°C) are required. Temperatures lower than 300°F or 150°C are seldom used for kebab grilling. To determine how hot your grill is, try the "palm test." Hold the palm of your hand about 5 inches (13 cm) from the heat source. If you can hold it there for not more than 2–3 seconds, the fire is HOT; for not more than 3–4 seconds, the fire is MEDIUM; and for at least 6–7 seconds, the fire is LOW. Many modern grills are equipped with a built-in temperature gauge or probe.

Since kebabs take a relatively short time to cook, it is important to organize everything from basting liquids and brushes to gloves, tongs, spatula and other tools beforehand. Fireproof oven mitts are absolutely essential when handling hot metal skewers. Whether using charcoal or gas, always ensure that there is sufficient fuel supply. It is most frustrating and often embarrassing to run out of fuel in the middle of cooking.

Cooking Time

ONE CAN ONLY APPROXIMATE THE COOKING time for kebabs since it depends on the source and intensity of heat, fuel used, type of grill, characteristics and size of meat, type of marinade and seasoning used. Cooking times provided throughout this book are estimates and guides; experiment with your own grill to find the best cooking time for a particular recipe. It is a distinct advantage if the grill is equipped with multiple burners (gas grills) or the grill rack can be moved up or down (charcoal grills) to position kebabs at a desired heat level. Since the cooking time will vary according to the size and type of kebabs, test the kebabs for doneness to make sure that they are cooked to your liking.

See the following chart for a rough guide to cooking times for the various sizes and types of meat kebabs; the times shown are total cooking time, including turning and basting.

APPROXIMATE COOKING TIME FOR THE VARIOUS TYPES AND SIZES OF KEBABS
[1 inch = 2.5 cm/1½ inches = 4 cm]

MEAT TYPE	SIZE	FIRE TEMP.	COOKING TIME	DONENESS
Beef cubes	1 inch	hot	6–8 min	medium-rare
	1½ inches	hot	8–10 min	medium-rare
Lamb cubes	1 inch	medium-hot	8–10 min	medium
	1½ inches	medium-hot	10–12 min	medium
Pork cubes	1 inch	medium	8–10 min	no longer pink
	1½ inches	medium	10–12 min	no longer pink
Chicken breast	1 inch	medium	4–6 min	no longer pink
	1½ inches	medium	6–8 min	no longer pink
Chicken thigh	1 inch	medium	6–8 min	no longer pink
	1½ inches	medium	8–10 min	no longer pink
Turkey breast	1 inch	medium	8–10 min	no longer pink
	1½ inch	medium	10–12 min	no longer pink
Turkey thigh	1 inch	medium	8–10 min	no longer pink
	1½ inches	medium	10–12min	no longer pink
Fish	1 inch	medium	4–6 min	opaque/flaky
	1½ inches	medium	6–8 min	opaque/flaky
Shrimps		medium	4–6 min	turn pink
Scallops		medium	6–8 min	turn opaque

Cooking Techniques

MEAT, POULTRY AND FISH KEBABS

The secret to a good kebab lies not only in marinating with the proper balance of herbs, spices, oil and acidity but also in cooking the meat to perfection. Meat, poultry and fish kebabs should be brought to room temperature before grilling and it is preferable to have meat kebabs cut into roughly equal sizes to ensure uniform and quick cooking. When threading pieces of meat onto a skewer, leave small spaces between them so heat can circulate around each piece. If meat pieces are pressed close together, they are likely to be steamed instead of being grilled. Because of their size, kebabs cook quickly. Cooking time varies with the kebab size but seldom exceeds 10 minutes. Turning kebabs frequently while grilling ensures even cooking, which should result in meat that is slightly crusty and charred on the outside but moist and tender inside. The seared crust that forms when the meat is exposed to direct heat gives the kebabs their characteristic smoky grilled flavor.

SATAYS AND YAKITORI

East Asian kebabs such as satays and yakitori, where smaller cuts or thin strips of meat are threaded onto bamboo skewers, are traditionally grilled over a special long, narrow charcoal firebox without any grate. Regular charcoal or gas grills can be used for grilling satays and yakitori without fear of them falling through the grate by placing the skewered meat on a flat perforated rack that rests on the regular grate. The small holes permit the flames and smoke through and are ideal for grilling seafood and vegetables; they are commonly available in stores that carry barbecue supplies. Another method is to put aluminum foil over one end of the grate and to place the exposed half of the bamboo skewer over the foil, and the meat-covered portion over direct heat. This

prevents the skewer from burning. Total cooking time for satays and yakitori is short and varies from 3 to 6 minutes depending upon the meat used; it is therefore a good idea to expose as much surface as possible to direct heat. I always baste satays while cooking with a mixture of vegetable oil and water or coconut milk, which not only produces the "sizzle factor" and prevents the meat from drying out, but also provides a charred smoky flavor resulting from limited flare-ups.

VEGETABLES

Mixing colorful vegetables with meat on a skewer looks good, but the results are not always what one desires. There is nothing more frustrating than to be served an attractive skewered lamb or beef kebab interspersed with an array of colorful vegetables only to find that either the meat is undercooked and the vegetables are perfectly grilled or the meat is perfectly cooked and the vegetables are charred. Vegetables and meats have different cooking times, so it is better to grill them on separate skewers. But if you are cooking meat and vegetables on the same skewer, choose firm vegetables such as green and red peppers, onion, zucchini, carrots, baby corn, celery, fennel, broccoli with its stem or eggplant. These vegetables are perfectly edible if undercooked but if slightly overcooked, their lightly charred flavor enhances the taste of the kebabs. Avoid combining mushrooms, tomatoes or fruits with meat on a skewer because after grilling they tend to become a soggy mess.

When grilling vegetables, cut them in large enough pieces 1½–2 inches (4–5 cm) that they do not slip through the grill into the fire. Vegetables require a medium to medium-low temperature but watch that they do not overcook. A combination of grilled red onion wedges and multicolored bell peppers or zucchini not only complements the taste of any kebab preparation it also creates a colorful presentation. For best results, microwave firm vegetable pieces for a few seconds, then marinate in a mixture of olive oil and your favorite herbs for a few minutes before threading onto skewers. Metal grill baskets or grilling trays with small holes are particularly useful for grilling and turning vegetables and seafood.

About Meats

ANY CUT OF MEAT, BE IT BEEF, PORK, LAMB, veal or poultry, is suitable for making kebabs. Tender cuts of meat do not require any special treatment except proper seasoning after the meat is cooked. Small pieces of fat or bacon inserted between lean meat pieces help baste the kebabs as they cook. Less tender cuts require proper marinating before cooking: the acidic component of the marinade helps to tenderize the meat by softening muscle fibers and connective tissue.

As a rule, pieces of meat for kebabs should be of roughly equal size, varying from 1 inch to 1½ inches (2.5–4 cm) but never over 2½ inches (6 cm). The smaller pieces or thin strips, used mostly in satays and yakitori, ensure quick cooking, and the constant turning and basting ensures even cooking without drying out the meat. It is preferable to use fresh meat, poultry and fish for kebabs, but if using frozen meats, thaw them in a refrigerator, particularly during warm summer months when grilling activity is at its peak.

Lamb

LAMB IS BY FAR THE MOST POPULAR MEAT FOR kebabs and is particularly relished in most countries around the Mediterranean, the Aegean region, the Balkans, the Middle East, and Central and South Asia. It is regarded as a perfect meat for grilling because it is well marbled with fat, has its own unique flavor and texture and can be grilled without the use of tenderizers or marinades. Loin is the tenderest portion of lamb; the leg is the second most tender portion and is a preferred cut for making kebabs. When using other cuts such as sirloin and shoulder chops, trim off the excess fat and marinate well to soften the tissue. Lamb requires a short cooking time; overcooking makes it chewy and dry. Cook over high or medium-high heat depending on the size of the kebabs; frequent basting with oil or melted butter during grilling keeps them moist and succulent.

Beef

TENDER BEEF CUTS, LIKE TENDERLOIN, FILET mignon, strip loin and rib-eye require a very short cooking time with little or no marinating. Less tender cuts, such as top sirloin, inside and outside round, sirloin tip, cross rib, rump or blade, must be marinated to tenderize the meat. For flavor and tenderness, grill over high heat for 3–5 minutes per side for medium rare and for 6–7 minutes per side for medium doneness. Cooking beef kebabs for longer than 10 minutes per side is likely to render them dry and chewy.

Pork

PORK IS NOT CONSIDERED AN IDEAL MEAT FOR kebabs because of its bland taste compared to beef or lamb and its tendency to dry out when grilled. Furthermore, there are religious taboos against eating pork in some cultures. Tender cuts of pork like fillet or tenderloin are not recommended for kebabs as they lack fat marbling and need to be heavily basted with oil during grilling to avoid drying out. The best cut for pork kebabs are loin and leg, but they must be well marinated with sufficient oil. Pork kebabs should be cooked until no longer pink in the center, so grilling on medium heat is recommended.

Poultry

AMONG POULTRY, CHICKEN IS UNFAILINGLY popular because of its availability, relatively low cost and ability to absorb the flavor of marinades and sauces. The breast meat tends to dry out during cooking unless well marinated in an oily marinade. Thighs are more flavorful, moist and dense and they are my choice for chicken kebabs.

Duck and turkey meat can also be used for kebabs but they require extra care with marinades. Turkey breast meat is dry and requires an oil-rich marinade or frequent basting with oil during grilling. Duck meat has a strong flavor and is oilier than turkey or chicken; it requires a more acidic marinade with less oil.

Medium to medium-high heat is recommended for grilling poultry kebabs since they are prone to drying out if cooked over high heat. White and dark poultry meat require different cooking times—the former cooks faster than the latter. It is therefore important to keep an eye on grilling and remove kebabs as soon as they are done.

Fish and Shellfish

FIRM-FLESHED FISH, SUCH AS HALIBUT, swordfish, tuna, monkfish, mahi mahi, ling cod, rockfish, grouper and turbot are ideal for kebabs; they retain their shape and do not flake or crumble easily while grilling. Less firm fish, such as salmon, cod, haddock, sea bass and snapper, have a tendency to flake and require special handling, such as using two skewers instead of one or grilling on a flat perforated rack. Shellfish like shrimps and sea scallops make easy and attractive kebabs; they are threaded whole onto a skewer and require a very short grilling time. Molluscs such as mussels, oysters, squids and octopus can be threaded onto a skewer and grilled on a mesh grate. Fish and shellfish have a delicate texture and are marinated only for a short period to avoid toughening up or "cooking" of muscles.

How Much Meat to Buy?

KEBABS ARE TRIMMED TO REMOVE UNDESIRable skin, bone, fat and gristle, so it is important to determine how much meat or poultry will provide the quantity of boneless meat required for kebabs. For example, a 4-lb (2-kg) leg of lamb, after removing bone, fat and unwanted tissue, would yield approximately 2½ lb (1.2 kg) of meat. This amount when cut into 1¼–1½ inches (3–4 cm) pieces will yield 50–60 kebabs. Assuming a normal main course serving of 10–12 pieces per person, this should be sufficient for 5–6 people. Similar estimates can be made with other cuts of meat. If kebabs are to be served as an appetizer, plan on about ¼ lb (125 g) of trimmed meat per person; if served as a main course, plan on no more than ½ lb (250 g) of trimmed meat per person.

Presentation and serving sizes vary, but a general rule of thumb for appetizers is to thread not more than four 1-inch (2.5-cm) kebabs on a short 4-inch (10-cm) or a 6-inch (15-cm) wooden or bamboo skewer. For a main course, two 10–12 inch long (25–30-cm) skewers with 4–6 kebabs each should suffice for one person.

The following chart lists the approximate number of different sized kebabs from boneless cuts of beef, lamb, poultry and fish as a general guide in deciding the serving size and amount of meat needed.

KEBAB SIZE AND APPROXIMATE NUMBER OF PIECES PER UNIT WEIGHT OF MEAT

KEBAB SIZE	1 LB (500 G)
1 inch (2.5 cm)	30
1¼ inches (3 cm)	25
1½ inches (4 cm)	20

About Marinating

MARINATING IS AN IMPORTANT ELEMENT OF kebab cookery. Marinades not only help tenderize and soften the meat but also add flavor, character and moisture. A typical marinade consists of three components—acid, fat and aromatic seasoning. the acid can be lemon or lime juice, vinegar, wine or fruit juice—all of which provide tart taste and flavor and help to tenderize the meat by changing the protein structure. The fat can be oil, butter, yogurt, sour cream or coconut milk. It provides moisture for the meat and balances the acidic component of the marinade. The presence of fat in the marinade provides the characteristic smoky aroma when it drips onto the hot fire and helps to brown the meat during grilling. The primary function of the aromatic component is to impart a unique flavor and character through the use of an assortment of herbs and spices.

Marinating improves the flavor of kebabs, but there are no hard and fast rules about marinating time. In general, the longer the cuts of meat are immersed in a marinade, the better the flavor. You can, however, over-marinate and run the risk of acid in the marinade literally "cooking" the meat, giving it a rubbery texture and an unattractive grayish appearance. The secret of successful marinating is to use the right amount of acid and to match the marinating time to the food. Foods have different optimum marinating times. For instance, fish, shellfish and vegetables require 30 minutes to 3 hours of marinating time, beyond which they start to cook, whereas, lamb, beef, pork and chicken can take 3 to 24 hours of marinating. Marinating time also depends on size: the larger the kebab, the longer the marinating time. Marinating overnight in the refrigerator is adequate for lamb, beef, pork and poultry kebabs.

Some ingredients, such as yogurt, buttermilk, papaya, pineapple, kiwi fruit, fig, ginger and melon, release efficient enzymes that are meat-tenderizing agents. Known as proteolytic enzymes, they digest or break down muscle fibers and connective tissue and cause the meat to become softer and more tender. When using any of these ingredients in a marinade, reduce the marinating time so the meat does not become mushy. The practice of using grated onion or onion juice in the marinade for kebabs in the Middle East is also said to help tenderize the meat.

Small quantities of sugar and salt balance the acidic edge of a marinade. Salt is said to draw out the juices from the meat and some authors recommend that it be omitted from the marinade and sprinkled over the meat during or after grilling. In my experience, the presence or absence of salt in the marinade makes no difference to the taste or texture of the final product.

Lean red meats, pork and poultry require a generous proportion of oils or fats in the marinade, whereas well-marbled cuts of beef and lamb can be grilled with a little oil or fat. Lean fish such as cod, haddock, halibut and monkfish, require oil-rich marinades, whereas oily fish like salmon, mackerel and tuna need less.

Marinades containing sugar, honey, molasses and sweet sauces are not appropriate for kebabs larger than 1 inch (2.5 cm) because the marinade will caramelize and burn before the meat is cooked. An alternative is to baste the meat with the marinade toward the end of cooking to minimize burning and ensure an attractive glaze. A small amount of sugar in the marinade helps soften the texture of meat by breaking down protein and changing the cell structure.

The acid in a marinade reacts with metals, so always use non-reactive containers of glass, ceramic, plastic or stainless steel when marinating. Never use aluminum containers. If marinating for more than an hour, food should be kept in a refrigerator.

As a rule, the marinade should be discarded after prolonged contact with uncooked meat. Most of the recipes included in this book use leftover marinade for basting purpose during grilling. This is a generally safe practice provided the kebabs are marinated overnight in the refrigerator and then grilled over direct medium or high heat, sufficient to destroy any bacterial flora that may have developed in the basting liquid. However, if the marinating time exceeds 12 hours in the refrigerator, either extra marinade for basting should be set aside at the very beginning or used marinade should be boiled for at least 2 minutes before using it for basting or as a sauce.

Selecting a marinade is a matter of personal preference and taste, and each geographical region has its own characteristic marinade and local or ethnic seasoning. In eastern and northern Europe, seasoning is used sparingly in marinades, either due to a lack of easy availability of herbs and spices or to a preference for not altering the natural flavor of the grilled meat. In Bulgaria, Albania and parts of the former Yugoslavia, marinades consist predominantly of olive oil and vinegars with little or no seasoning, and this also holds true to some extent in Ukraine, Georgia and the southern part of Russia. Throughout the Mediterranean and the Middle East, marinades are simple, consisting of olive oil, lemon juice, onion juice and few herbs and spices. As one moves from the Middle East toward Iran and the Indian subcontinent, the use of spices and herbs in the marinades increases dramatically.

In Asia, each region is characterized by its use of distinctive herbs and spices in marinades. For example, throughout the Indian subcontinent, cumin, coriander, cloves, cinnamon, nutmeg, chilies, turmeric, ginger and garlic are mixed with yogurt and lemon juice. The most complex array of herbs and spices used in marinades is to be found in Southeast Asian countries. There lemon grass, lime, galangal, white pepper, lime leaves, basil, chilies, cumin, turmeric, coconut milk and fish sauce are fairly common. In Japan, a combination of Japanese soy sauce, mirin, sake, miso and sugar is used both as a marinade and as a dipping sauce. Koreans like their beef marinated in a mixture of soy sauce, sugar, garlic, sesame oil and some chilies. Chinese marinades contain soy sauce, five-spice powder, ginger, garlic and sesame oil.

In Latin America, wherever marinades are used, they tend to be fiery hot. Chilies are an essential ingredient of South American and Mexican marinades and several varieties, such as hontaka or mirasol chilies, ancho chili pepper, poblano peppers, jalapeño peppers and chipotle peppers, are used to provide the necessary heat. Other ingredients include lime juice, red wine vinegar, cilantro, thyme, oregano, marjoram and cumin. In the Caribbean, marinades include habanero or scotch bonnet chili peppers, lime juice, brown sugar, allspice, curry powder, marjoram and a variety of other herbs. In the Spanish Caribbean islands of Cuba, Puerto Rico and Dominican Republic, meats and seafood are most often marinated in a tangy marinade called adobo made with cumin, garlic, sour orange juice, lime juice, oregano, chilies and turmeric. African marinades include the ubiquitous Maggi seasoning, garlic, ginger, chilies, vinegar and roasted peanut powder and often curry powder.

A mixture of dried herbs and spices called "rubs" may be used to coat meat before grilling or sprinkled over it after grilling. The use of rubs is not common for kebabs because dry herbs and spices clinging to the outside of meat tend to burn when grilled directly over a hot fire. It is not uncommon, however, to enhance the flavor by sprinkling a mixture of selected herbs and spices over kebabs after they are cooked. For example, throughout the Middle East it is common to sprinkle cooked kebabs before serving with *baharat* or a sour seasoning called *sumac* made from dry powdered berries. Likewise, in South Asia an array of aromatic powdered spices collectively known as *masala* is sprinkled over kebabs to enhance the flavor of the grilled meat.

Sauces are often used to complement or enhance the taste and flavor of grilled meat either during cooking or soon after. Some of these sauces, such as barbecue or teriyaki sauce, are referred to as finishing sauces. Because of their high sugar content, which is prone to burning while grilling, they are brushed over the meat toward the end of cooking to provide color and an attractive shiny glaze to the finished food. Other sauces such as Southeast Asian peanut sauce, Indian yogurt *raita* or mint chutney, North African *harissa* and *charmoula sauces*, South American *chimichurri* sauce, and Vietnamese *nuoc mam*, accompany cooked satays or kebabs. Then there is a whole variety of dipping sauces popular in Southeast Asia and East Asia used for enhancing taste and flavor by dipping cooked skewered meat in them before serving.

About Skewers

SKEWERS ARE AN INDISPENSABLE PART OF kebab cookery. They come in different sizes and shapes and are made of metal, wood or bamboo. They range from thin 4-inch (10-cm) long bamboo sticks you can throw away to oversize, hand-beaten, iron skewers that can exceed 3 feet (90 cm), commonly used in Persian and Indian tandoori cooking.

Metal skewers are a wise investment: they can be used repeatedly, are easy to clean and the grilled food slides off them easily. They range from 6 to 18 inches (15 to 45 cm) in length and from ⅛ inch to 1 inch (0.3 to 2.5 cm) in width and can be flat, round or square. Flat or square skewers are recommended for kebabs that involve wrapping ground meat around the skewer; during grilling the meat is less likely to fall off. The ground meat is wrapped around the skewer like a sausage and pressed on all down its length. The meat is not cooked on a metal grill but is suspended over the fire with either end of the skewer resting on the edge of the fire box. Another important reason for using this type of skewer for ground meat kebabs is that the heat is transferred through the hot metal, which helps cook the inside of the kebab while the outside is cooked by direct heat.

Large flat metal skewers made of iron, stainless steel or aluminum are popular throughout the Middle East and in Iran, whereas square 4-sided skewers made of cast iron are commonly used throughout the Indian subcontinent to cook ground meat kebabs.

Narrow metal skewers are used for grilling individual pieces of meat, poultry, fish and vegetables. Thick skewers may not be suitable for grilling firm vegetable and fruit pieces which tend to split when threaded onto such skewers. Thin metal or wooden skewers with sharp points work best for these foods. Decorative metal skewers available in different attractive styles from gourmet kitchen outlets can enhance the appearance of kebabs served in more formal settings. These may include unique circular skewers and skewers with ornate design heads.

Wooden or bamboo skewers are relatively inexpensive, easily available and disposable and are ideal for making kebabs for a large crowd. They are found throughout Southeast Asia and East Asia, are used for cooking smaller pieces of meat that require quick grilling such as satays and yakitori, and range from 4 to 12 inches (10 to 30 cm) in length. Wooden or bamboo skewers are not suited to pieces of meat larger than 1 inch (2.5 cm) because they require a longer cooking time that may burn the skewers and impart undesirable flavors to the food.

To minimize the burning of wooden skewers, either thread meat and vegetable pieces onto the entire length of the skewer or keep any exposed portion of the skewer away from direct heat. One way to do this is to place a strip of foil over one edge of the grill and place the exposed end of the skewers on that. Presoaking wooden or bamboo skewers for 30 minutes or so in water also minimizes burning. The narrow fire boxes for grilling satays and yakitori common in Asia prevent wooden skewers burning, since only the meat-bearing end of the skewer is exposed to direct fire. Wooden or bamboo skewers are unsuitable for cooking seasoned ground meat because of the long time required for such kebab cooking and the possibility of burning the skewers.

Metal skewers are best for meat pieces larger than 1 inch (2.5 cm). They can hold more weight and are easier to work with. In some instances, there may be a need to use two parallel skewers together to prevent spinning and sliding of food while grilling. This is particularly true when grilling vegetables that tend to soften after cooking (for example, whole tomatoes and mushrooms) and in some cases poultry or fish.

Although the size of skewers used is a matter of availability and personal preference, for appetizer servings, short skewers, 4 to 6 inches (10 to 15 cm) long, are ideal; for individual main course servings, medium size skewers, 8 to 10 inches (20 to 25 cm), or long skewers, 10 to 12 inches (25 to 30 cm), are suitable. Skewers longer than 12 inches (30 cm) are generally used when cooking for a crowd.

A most useful and relatively inexpensive contraption is a shish kebab rack, which consists of a metal frame that is placed over the grill. The frame is provided with notches in which 6 metal skewers can be firmly held and turned over with ease when one side is cooked.

Europe

Western and Eastern

Although kebab cookery is well established in southern and eastern Europe, it has failed to make any significant inroads in western and northern Europe. In Belgium, Austria, Switzerland and the Scandinavian countries it is difficult to find any type of kebab, other than a few Indonesian restaurants serving satays or small eateries run by Turkish immigrants. In the United Kingdom, kebabs have gained acceptance and popularity as a fast food thanks to over 20,000 kebab shops operated by Turkish, Lebanese, Indian, Pakistani and Bangladeshi expatriates. Kebabs are becoming a part of British drinking culture and are increasingly available in British pubs. A newly established National Association of Kebab Shops aims to safeguard the integrity of the kebab industry in the UK by setting standards and encouraging improvements. In fact, kebabs are not far behind traditional fish and chips and pizza as favorite fast foods in the UK.

Southern European countries bordering the Mediterranean Sea, such as Spain, France, Italy and Greece, have their own distinctive kebabs. Portugal, unlike Spain, has no Mediterranean exposure but its cuisine remains remarkably similar to that of Spain as far as kebabs are concerned. The area surrounding the Mediterranean Sea has been colonized by Phoenicians, Romans, Greeks and Turks and many of the cuisines developed in this region reflect not only the lingering influence of the colonizers, but also the culinary contributions made by North African and Arab countries. Because of a lack of suitable grazing land throughout this region, cattle farming is rare. Beef has to be imported and is rather expensive, but lamb, goat, pork, poultry, game, fish and shellfish are favorite meats for kebabs. In general, pork is popular in the western Mediterranean (Spain), poultry and veal in the central Mediterranean (France, Italy), lamb in eastern and southern Mediterranean (Greece, Turkey, Morocco, Tunisia, Algeria, Lebanon) and fish and shellfish throughout the region.

Wine, fresh herbs and olive oil are central to the cuisine of Mediterranean Europe. In Italy kebabs are called *spiedini* and are usually marinated in wine, olive oil, garlic, oregano and rosemary. In France they are referred to as *brochettes* and the preferred seasoning is wine, olive oil, garlic, thyme and rosemary. Greeks like their *souvlaki* marinated in wine, lemon juice, olive oil and garlic; herbs such as bay leaf, flat-leaf parsley, oregano, rosemary, dill and basil are commonly used.

Throughout Greece, souvlaki or *souvlakia* are as popular as hamburgers are in North America. Although there are chicken and pork souvlaki, the preferred meat is leg of lamb. Souvlaki cooked on small wooden skewers without any vegetables are known as *kalamakia*, a typical Greek street food that can be eaten on the run with or without bread. Souvlaki with larger pieces of meat and vegetables threaded onto longer skewers are called *merida* and are served in more established eating places. In Athens local souvlaki houses are called *souvlat-zidiko* and serve both elaborate sit-down souvlaki dinners and takeout souvlaki or *kalamaki* sandwiches—souvlaki wrapped in a heated pita bread with onion, tomato and tzatziki sauce. Ground beef souvlaki known as *beefteki* is also popular takeout fare but Athenians prefer lamb and pork souvlaki.

In Spain, skewered grilled kebabs are called *pinchos* or *pinchitos* and tend to be spicy, reflecting the Moorish culinary influence. Moors dominated Spain from the 8th to the 12th century and had a profound influence on Spanish art, architecture, culture and cuisine, particularly in the Andalusian region. It was natural that the Moorish fondness for grilled meat on skewers found a foothold in Spain in the form of *pinchitos morunos*. They are identical to Moroccan kebabs, the only difference being that instead of lamb, pinchitos are usually made of pork as there is no religious taboo against it in Spain.

Portuguese and Spanish explorers, returning from the Far East with exotic spices, radically changed the regional cuisines of Spain and Portugal. Today's spicy grilled *pinchitos* and *palillos* are favorite items in the tapas bars of Spain. The Portuguese have been particularly adept at absorbing culinary traditions from other colonized countries. Herbs and spices from India, the Far East, Africa and South America continue to make Portuguese cuisine quite different from that found in neighboring countries bordering the Mediterranean. Although grilled fish and beef are popular throughout Portugal, on the Island of Madeira skewered grilled beef, known as *espetada*, has become an integral part of the traditional cuisine.

In eastern Europe, kebab culture flourishes and is attributed to strong Turkish and Persian culinary influences. Romanian, Albanian, Bulgarian and the cuisines of other Balkan countries show more affinity with their Turkish neighbors than with Russia. In Romania, kebabs are called *raznijici* and ground meat kebabs are referred to as *lule*, a term borrowed from the Middle East. Inhabitants of the former Yugoslavia call their kebabs *cebapcici* or *cevapcici* and despite any political and ethnic differences, these are popular with Serbs, Croats and Bosnians alike. Bulgarians refer to them as *shish kebap* and

Albanians as *shish qebab*, reflecting their Turkish heritage. In Poland kebabs are referred to as *szaszlyk*, and *szaszlyki z kielbasa* (a skewer threaded with slices of kielbasa sausage alternating with onion slices and bacon pieces) grilled over an open fire is a favorite street food.

Georgian, Armenian and Azerbaijani foods have many similarities and this is particularly true of kebab cookery. Armenia is not well known to outsiders and it has endured many upheavals and changes to its boundaries throughout its history. Its cuisine reflects ties with Turkey, Iran and Russia and to some extent Greece, one of the reasons that a wide variety of kebabs is offered in this small country. Kebabs are referred to as *shashlik, kebab, shish kebab*, as well as by their typical Armenian name *khorovatz* or *khorovadz,* and a variety of meats, such as beef, mutton, chicken and pork are combined on the same skewer. The meat is seasoned with thyme, coriander, red pepper flakes, black pepper and occasionally red wine, tomato paste and wine vinegar in the marinade.

In neighboring Azerbaijan, kebabs reflect their Turkish and Central Asian influence, and allspice and nutmeg are preferred seasonings. Ground meat kebabs called *lyulya* and lamb shish kebabs are sold from roadside stalls in Baku, but the most prized kebab is sturgeon served with a pomegranate sauce called *narsharab.*

Shish kebabs known as *shashlyk* found their way into Russia from Armenia and Georgia, which were until recently part of the former Soviet Union. Restaurants specializing in *shashlyk* have sprung up all over major cities in Russia and are called *shashlychnayas.* In Moscow, the best *shashlyk* is reported to be from Aragvi Restaurant, which is well known for its Georgian cuisine. The word *shashlyk* appears to have originated from *shashka* which means sword in Georgia. Georgians as a rule do not use many herbs and spices as seasoning for their kebabs and prefer freshly slaughtered lamb. A classic Georgian preparation called *mtsvadi* alternates pieces of young lamb with fat, onion and tomatoes on a dagger-like skewer called *shampuri.* They are grilled over hot coals without any marinating. *Mtsvadi* is sprinkled with ground barberries and served with the Georgian bread *lavashi,* tomatoes, cucumber and chopped onion. Another Georgian favorite is *basturma*; less tender cuts of lamb or beef are marinated in a mixture of red wine and pomegranate juice, threaded onto metal skewers with or without vegetables and grilled over an open fire, then liberally sprinkled with fresh mint and cilantro. *Basturma*, although Georgian in origin, is served all over the Caucasus.

SHISH KEBABS

Shish Qebab

SERVES 6

Marinade

½ cup • 125 mL	olive oil
2 Tbsp • 25 mL	red wine vinegar
2 tsp • 10 mL	dried oregano
3	bay leaves, crushed
1 tsp • 5 mL	salt
½ tsp • 2.5 mL	freshly ground black pepper

Kebabs

2 lb • 1 kg	boneless lamb, beef or pork, cut into 1-inch (2.5-cm) pieces
2	medium onions, quartered and layers separated
12	medium metal or presoaked bamboo skewers

1 Combine all marinade ingredients. Add meat pieces and toss well to coat. Marinate in the refrigerator for at least 4 hours, but preferably overnight.

2 Drain marinade and reserve. Thread 4–5 pieces of meat alternating with onion onto each skewer.

3 Grill over medium-high heat for about 8–10 minutes, turning and basting with reserved marinade often.

4 Serve with rice pilaf or salad.

LAMB KEBABS

Karski Shashlik

Marinade

½ cup • 125 mL	dry red wine
¼ cup • 50 mL	olive oil
3 Tbsp • 45 mL	chopped fresh parsley
2 Tbsp • 25 mL	lemon juice
1	medium onion, finely chopped
1 Tbsp • 15 mL	tomato paste
1 tsp • 5 mL	garlic paste
1 tsp • 5 mL	dried oregano
1½ tsp • 7.5 mL	salt
2	bay leaves, crushed
½ tsp • 2.5 mL	freshly ground black pepper
½ tsp • 2.5 mL	red pepper flakes

Kebabs

2 lb • 1 kg	boneless leg of lamb, excess fat removed, cut into 1½-inch (4-cm) cubes
2	medium red onions, quartered and layers separated
2	green bell peppers, seeded and cut into 1-inch (2.5-cm) squares
8	Italian plum tomatoes, cut in half
8	long metal skewers

1 In a non-reactive bowl, combine all marinade ingredients. Add lamb pieces and toss well to coat thoroughly. Cover and marinate in the refrigerator for at least 4 hours, or preferably overnight.

2 Drain marinade and reserve. Thread about 5–6 pieces of lamb on each of 4 skewers. Thread onion, green pepper and tomato on separate remaining skewers. Brush all skewers liberally with reserved marinade.

3 Grill skewers over medium-high heat, turning and basting frequently with marinade. Remove vegetable skewers when slightly charred and lamb skewers when outside is evenly brown on all sides and inside is pink. Allow to rest for 5 minutes.

4 Serve over rice or bulgar pilaf.

PORK KEBABS
Khorovadz Khori Miss

Also known as karabakh khorovats, these kebabs are an Armenian specialty and are served with a piquant pomegranate sauce called *narsharab* (see page 230). These kebabs do not require any marinating.

SERVES 4

1 tsp • 5 mL	salt
1 tsp • 5 mL	freshly ground black pepper
2 lb • 1 kg	boneless pork loin, cut into 1½-inch (4-cm) cubes
¼ cup • 50 mL	olive oil
4	long metal skewers
3	medium tomatoes, cut into 8 wedges
2	green onions, sliced finely
	pomegranate sauce (*narsharab*)

1 Sprinkle salt and black pepper over pork cubes in a bowl and let rest for 30 minutes.

2 Thread about 10 pieces of pork onto each skewer, and brush with olive oil.

3 Grill skewers over medium heat for about 15 minutes, turning and basting frequently with oil, until meat is evenly brown on all sides.

4 Slide meat off skewers onto individual plates and garnish with sliced green onion and tomato wedges.

5 Serve with pomegranate sauce in separate small bowls.

Ground LAMB KEBABS

Luleh Kebab or *Keyma Kebab*

SERVES 4–8

2 lb • 1 kg	lean ground lamb
1	large onion, finely chopped
1 cup • 250 mL	finely chopped fresh Italian parsley
1 cup • 250 mL	finely chopped fresh mint
1	egg, lightly beaten
1 tsp • 5 mL	ground coriander
1 tsp • 5 mL	ground cumin
1 tsp • 5 mL	salt
½ tsp • 2.5 mL	freshly ground black pepper
2 Tbsp • 25 mL	melted butter for basting
8	green onions, thinly sliced
2	medium tomatoes, cut into 8 wedges
8	long metal skewers, preferably flat

1. Combine lamb, chopped onion, half the parsley and mint, egg, coriander, cumin, salt and black pepper in a large bowl. Knead with hands until well mixed. Cover and refrigerate overnight to let flavors to develop.

2. Wet hands and wrap portions of meat mixture around each skewer to form a sausage-like shape, about 4 inches (10 cm) long and 1 inch (2.5 cm) in diameter. Try to have at least 2 sausages per skewer.

3. Grill over high heat, turning frequently so meat browns evenly on all sides, about 10–12 minutes. When done, brush kebabs with melted butter.

4. Remove kebabs from skewers and serve hot. Garnish with mixture of sliced green onions, remaining chopped parsley and mint, and tomato wedges.

FISH KEBABS

Tsougov Shish Kebab

SERVES 5

Marinade

¼ cup • 50 mL	lemon juice
¼ cup • 50 mL	grated onion
¼ cup • 50 mL	olive oil
1 tsp • 5 mL	salt
½ tsp • 2.5 mL	freshly ground black pepper

Kebabs

2 lb • 1 kg	firm fish fillets, such as halibut, swordfish, tuna or mahi mahi, cut into 1-inch (2.5-cm) cubes
several	bay leaves
10	medium metal or pre soaked wooden skewers
¼ cup • 50 mL	melted butter for basting
½ cup • 125 mL	chopped green onion
¼ cup • 50 mL	chopped fresh parsley
2	medium tomatoes, cut into 8 wedges
2	lemons, cut into wedges

1 Combine marinade ingredients in a non-reactive bowl. Toss fish pieces and bay leaves gently in marinade to coat. Cover and let stand for 2 hours at room temperature, stirring occasionally.

2 Remove fish and bay leaves from marinade and thread about 5–6 pieces of fish alternating with bay leaves onto each skewer.

3 Grill skewers over medium heat for about 8–10 minutes, turning and basting frequently with melted butter.

4 Transfer fish onto individual plates, garnish with green onion, parsley, tomato and lemon wedges.

5 Serve with plain or saffron rice pilaf (recipe page 219).

CHICKEN KEBAB

Djudja Kabab

Marinade

1 cup • 250 mL	**sour cream**
2 Tbsp • 25 mL	**finely chopped onion**
1 Tbsp • 15 mL	**pomegranate sauce** *(narsharab, page 230)*
1 Tbsp • 15 mL	**finely chopped parsley**
1 tsp • 5 mL	**ground allspice**
1 tsp • 5 mL	**salt**
½ tsp • 2.5 mL	**ground nutmeg**
½ tsp • 2.5 mL	**freshly ground black pepper**

Kebabs

2 lb • 1 kg	**boneless, skinless chicken thighs, cut into 1½-inch (4-cm) pieces**
8	**medium metal skewers**
	sumac **(see page 233), sliced lemon and cilantro for garnish**

1. In a non-reactive bowl, combine all marinade ingredients. Add chicken pieces and toss gently to coat. Cover and marinate in the refrigerator for at least 4 hours, but preferably overnight.

2. Remove chicken, reserving marinade. Thread 5–6 chicken pieces onto each skewer.

3. Grill over medium heat about 3 minutes per side, turning and basting with reserved marinade frequently.

4. Sprinkle kebabs with sumac and serve with either rice pilaf (*plov*) or with traditional tandir or pita bread. Garnish with sumac, sliced lemon and cilantro leaves.

MUTTON KEBABS

Ovneshko Na Shish

These kebabs require no marinating and are simply seasoned with salt and pepper.

SERVES 6

2 lb • 1kg	**boneless leg of lamb, cut into 1¼-inch (3-cm) pieces**
4	**bacon strips, cut into 1-inch (2.5-cm) pieces**
2	**green or red bell peppers, seeded and cut into 1¼-inch (3-cm) squares**
2	**medium red onions, quartered, and layers separated**
12	**long metal skewers**
	salt and freshly ground black pepper
4	**medium tomatoes, each cut into 8 wedges**

1 Thread about 4–5 pieces of lamb alternating with bacon, bell pepper and onion onto each skewer.

2 Grill over medium-high heat for about 3–4 minutes per side, turning frequently to avoid burning. Lamb should be slightly charred on the outside but pink inside.

3 Season grilled kebabs with salt and pepper and cover with a lid or foil for about 5 minutes before serving.

4 Serve with tomato wedges and rice pilaf.

Grilled MUSSEL SKEWERS

Brochettes de Moules

These kebabs are popular around St. Tropez on the Mediterranean coast.

SERVES 4–6

2 lb • 1 kg	blue mussels (preferably cultured)
½ cup • 125 mL	white wine
1 tsp • 5 mL	chopped fresh thyme
1 tsp • 5 mL	minced garlic
4	strips bacon or lardoons (pork fat), cut in 1-inch (2.5-cm) pieces
1	egg beaten with 2 Tbsp (25 mL) milk
1 cup • 250 mL	dried breadcrumbs
2 Tbsp • 25 mL	olive oil
¼ cup • 50 mL	heavy cream
½ tsp • 2.5 mL	salt
½ tsp • 2.5 mL	freshly ground black pepper
12	presoaked medium wooden skewers

1 Scrub mussels well under cold water. Place in a pan with wine, thyme and garlic, cover and boil until mussels open. Strain liquid and reserve.

2 Remove mussels from shells, making sure all byssus threads or beards are pulled off mussel meats. Thread mussels alternately with bacon or lardoons pieces onto skewers.

3 Dip each skewer in egg mixture, then roll in breadcrumbs. Grill over medium heat for 2 minutes per side. Brush with olive oil between turns.

4 Boil reserved mussel liquid in a pan to reduce it by half. Add cream and continue boiling for 1–2 minutes. Add salt and pepper. Transfer sauce to a bowl.

5 Serve mussel skewers with sauce on the side.

SKEWERED BEEF

Boeuf en Brochette

SERVES 4 *Marinade*

¼ cup • 50 mL	**olive oil**
¼ cup • 50 mL	**melted butter**
¼ cup • 50 mL	**lemon juice**
1 Tbsp • 15 mL	**Dijon mustard**
1 tsp • 5 mL	**freshly ground black pepper**
1 tsp • 5 mL	**salt**
½ tsp • 2.5 mL	**hot pepper flakes**
½ tsp • 2.5 mL	**dried thyme**

Kebabs

2 lb • 1 kg	**beef tenderloin cut into 1½-inch (4-cm) cubes**
8	**long metal skewers**
1 tsp • 5 mL	**finely minced garlic**
½ tsp • 2.5 mL	**lemon juice**
2 Tbsp • 25 mL	**melted butter**

1 Combine marinade ingredients in a non-reactive bowl. Add beef cubes, toss well to coat each piece thoroughly. Cover and marinate in the refrigerator for at least 4 hours or preferably overnight.

2 Remove beef from marinade. Thread 5–6 pieces onto each skewer. Set aside for 10 minutes to reach room temperature.

3 Grill over high heat, turning and basting with leftover marinade frequently. Cook for not more than 3 minutes per side.

4 Mix garlic, lemon juice and melted butter. Before serving brush cooked kebabs with butter mixture.

5 Serve over rice or salad.

SKEWERED LAMB

Brochettes d' Agneau

Marinade

½ cup • 125 mL	olive oil
¼ cup • 50 mL	lemon juice
¼ cup • 50 mL	red wine
4	cloves garlic, finely minced
2	bay leaves, crushed
½ tsp • 2.5 mL	dried thyme
½ tsp • 2.5 mL	dried oregano
½ tsp • 2.5 mL	dried rosemary
½ tsp • 2.5 mL	freshly ground black pepper
1 tsp • 5 mL	salt

Kebabs

2 lb • 1 kg	boneless leg of lamb cut into 1-inch (2.5-cm) cubes
½ lb • 250 g	sliced bacon, cut crosswise into 1-inch (2.5-cm) pieces
2	medium red onions, quartered lengthwise and layers separated
2	green bell peppers, seeded and cut into 1-inch (2.5-cm) squares
12	long metal skewers

1 In a non-reactive bowl, combine all marinade ingredients. Add lamb cubes, toss well to coat, cover and marinate in the refrigerator for at least 6 hours, but preferably overnight.

2 Drain marinade and reserve. Thread 5–6 pieces of lamb alternating with bacon, onion and green pepper onto each skewer. Let rest for 10 minutes before grilling.

3 Grill on medium-high heat, turning and basting with reserved marinade occasionally, until meat is brown on outside and center remains pink, approximately 5 minutes per side.

4 Serve over rice pilaf.

CHICKEN KEBABS

Brochettes de Poulet

SERVES 6

Marinade

½ cup • 125 mL	olive oil
½ cup • 125 mL	white wine
2 Tbsp • 25 mL	lemon juice
3 Tbsp • 45 mL	honey
2 Tbsp • 25 mL	Dijon mustard
1 Tbsp • 15 mL	minced garlic
1 tsp • 5 mL	dried thyme
1 tsp • 5 mL	coarsely ground black pepper
½ tsp • 2.5 mL	salt

Kebabs

2 lb • 1 kg	chicken breasts, cut into 1¼-inch (3-cm) cubes
2	red or green bell peppers, seeded and cut into 1¼-inch (3-cm) squares
2	medium red onions, quartered and layers separated
12	long metal skewers
12	cherry tomatoes

1 Combine all marinade ingredients in a non-reactive bowl. Add chicken pieces and toss well to coat. Cover and marinate in refrigerator for at least 4 hours or preferably overnight.

2 Drain marinade and reserve. Thread 4–5 pieces of chicken alternating with bell pepper and onion onto each skewer.

3 Grill over medium heat, turning and basting with reserved marinade occasionally, about 10 minutes.

4 Thread a cherry tomato onto each skewer before serving.

5 Serve with rice or salad.

LAMB KEBABS

Shashlyk iz Baraniny

Marinade

1 cup • 250 mL	pomegranate juice
½ cup • 125 mL	red wine
¼ cup • 50 mL	olive oil
2 Tbsp • 25 mL	lemon juice
1	large onion, finely grated
1 Tbsp • 15 mL	chopped fresh parsley
1 Tbsp • 15 mL	chopped fresh basil
1 tsp • 5 mL	salt
1 tsp • 5 mL	freshly ground black pepper

Kebabs

2 lb • 1 kg	boneless leg of lamb, cut into 1½-inch (4-cm) pieces
8	medium metal skewers

1 In a large bowl, combine all marinade ingredients. Add lamb and toss to coat thoroughly. Cover and marinate for up to 2 days in refrigerator.

2 Drain marinade, boil for 2 minutes and reserve. Thread 5–6 lamb pieces onto each skewer.

3 Grill over medium-high heat, turning and basting with reserved marinade frequently, about 10 minutes.

4 Serve with onion and tomato salad.

BEEF KEBABS

Basturma

SERVES 5

Marinade

1 cup • 250 mL	pomegranate juice (*narsharab, page 230*)
1	medium onion, grated
¼ cup • 50 mL	olive oil
2 Tbsp • 25 mL	red wine vinegar
2 Tbsp • 25 mL	fresh chopped parsley
1 Tbsp • 15 mL	crushed coriander seeds
1 tsp • 5 mL	minced garlic
1 tsp • 5 mL	salt
½ tsp • 2.5 mL	freshly ground black pepper

Kebabs

2 lb • 1 kg	top sirloin beefsteak, cut into 1¼-inch (3-cm) pieces
10	long metal skewers
1	medium onion, quartered and layers separated
2	green bell peppers, seeded and cut into 1¼-inch (3-cm) squares
	chopped cilantro leaves for garnish

1 In a non-reactive bowl, mix all marinade ingredients. Add meat pieces and toss to coat thoroughly. Cover and marinate overnight in the refrigerator.

2 Drain marinade and reserve. Thread 4–5 pieces of beef alternating with onion and green pepper onto each skewer.

3 Grill skewers over high heat for about 3–5 minutes per side, turning and basting with reserved marinade at each turn.

4 Serve with lettuce and tomato sprinkled with chopped cilantro leaves.

LAMB KEBABS

Arni Souvlaki

Marinade

¼ cup • 50 mL	**dry white wine**
¼ cup • 50 mL	**olive oil**
2 Tbsp • 25 mL	**lemon juice**
1 Tbsp • 15 mL	**crushed garlic**
1 tsp • 5 mL	**dried oregano**
1 tsp • 5 mL	**salt**
½ tsp • 2.5 mL	**freshly ground black pepper**

Kebabs

2 lb • 1 kg	**boneless leg of lamb, cut into 1½-inch (4-cm) pieces**
several	**bay leaves**
10	**medium metal skewers**

1 Combine all marinade ingredients in a non-reactive bowl. Add lamb pieces and stir well to coat. Cover and marinate for 12 to 24 hours in the refrigerator.

2 Drain marinade and reserve. If marination exceeds 12 hours, boil reserved marinade for 2 minutes. Thread 4–5 lamb pieces alternating with bay leaves onto each skewer.

3 Grill over medium-high heat, turning and basting with reserved marinade frequently, about 12–15 minutes.

4 Serve with pita bread, tomatoes, lemon wedges and *tzatziki* (recipe page 222).

MIXED GRILL
Kokoretsi Souvlaki

SERVES 8

Marinade

1	small onion, grated
½ cup • 125 mL	olive oil
2 Tbsp • 25 mL	lemon juice
2 Tbsp • 25 mL	chopped fresh flat-leaf parsley
1 tsp • 5 mL	dried oregano
3	bay leaves, crushed
1 tsp • 5 mL	salt
½ tsp • 2.5 mL	freshly ground black pepper

Kebabs

½ lb • 250 g	lamb sweetbreads
2	fresh lemons
1 lb • 500 g	lamb liver
2	lamb hearts
2	lamb kidneys
several	bay leaves
16	short metal or presoaked bamboo skewers

1 Combine all marinade ingredients in a non-reactive bowl and set aside.

2 Rinse sweetbreads, place in a pan, add water to cover and juice of half a lemon. Boil for 2 minutes, drain. Add more cold water and juice of 1 lemon. Add liver, hearts, kidneys and sweetbread and soak for about 30 minutes.

3 Drain, remove membrane and fatty tissue and cut organs into 1¼-inch (3-cm) pieces.

4 Add meat pieces to marinade and toss well to coat thoroughly. Marinate for at least 2 hours in the refrigerator.

5 Drain marinade and reserve. Thread meats alternating with bay leaves onto each skewer. Brush with marinade.

6 Grill over medium-high heat, turning and basting with reserved marinade frequently, about 10–12 minutes or until cooked through. Serve as an appetizer.

Stuffed MEATBALL SKEWERS
Keftedakia

SERVES 8

2 lb • 1 kg	minced lamb or lean beef
½ cup • 125 mL	breadcrumbs
1	egg, beaten
1	medium onion, grated
1 Tbsp • 15 mL	minced garlic
1 tsp • 5 mL	salt
½ tsp • 2.5 mL	freshly ground black pepper
2 Tbsp • 25 mL	chopped flat-leaf parsley
1 Tbsp • 15 mL	chopped fresh mint leaves
1 tsp • 5 mL	dried oregano
2 Tbsp • 25 mL	lemon juice
	feta cheese cut into ½-inch (1.5-cm) squares
several	short presoaked bamboo skewers
	olive oil for basting

1 Mix ground meat, breadcrumbs, egg, onion, garlic, salt, pepper, parsley, mint, oregano and lemon juice. Knead mixture well by hand, cover and refrigerate for at least 4 hours or preferably overnight for flavors to develop.

2 Wet hands and make meatballs about 1½ inches (4 cm) in diameter. Insert a feta cheese square in the middle of each ball and roll ball back to its original shape.

3 Thread 2 meatballs onto each skewer, brush with olive oil and grill over high heat, turning constantly until golden brown on all sides, about 5 minutes.

4 Brush with olive oil and serve on a bed of lettuce as appetizers.

PORK KEBABS
Xirino Souvlaki

SERVES 5

Marinade

⅔ cup • 150 mL	olive oil
¼ cup • 50 mL	red wine vinegar or lemon juice
1	medium onion, grated
2–3	bay leaves (crushed)
2 tsp • 10 mL	dried oregano
2 tsp • 10 mL	crushed coriander seeds
1 tsp • 5 mL	salt
1 tsp • 5 mL	dried thyme
1 tsp • 5 mL	garlic paste
½ tsp • 2.5 mL	freshly ground black pepper

Kebabs

2 lb • 1 kg	lean boneless pork, cut into 1-inch (2.5-m) cubes
10	medium metal or presoaked bamboo skewers

1 Mix marinade ingredients in a non-reactive bowl. Add pork cubes and toss well to coat. Cover and refrigerate for up to 24 hours.

2 Drain marinade and reserve. If marination exceeds 12 hours boil reserved marinade for 2 minutes. Thread about 5–6 pieces of pork onto each skewer, leaving about ¼ inch (0.5 cm) space between each cube.

3 Grill over medium heat, turning and basting with reserved marinade, until meat is crusty and brown on the outside and juicy and succulent inside.

4 Serve with or without pita bread topped with sliced onion, tomatoes and *tzatziki* (recipe page 222).

SWORDFISH KEBABS

Xifias Souvlaki

Marinade

½ cup • 125 mL	**extra virgin olive oil**
¼ cup • 50 mL	**lemon juice**
2 tsp • 10 mL	**dried oregano**
1 tsp • 5 mL	**thyme**
1 tsp • 5 mL	**garlic paste**
1 tsp • 5 mL	**salt**
½ tsp • 2.5 mL	**freshly ground black pepper**

Kebabs

2 lb • 1 kg	**swordfish fillets cut into 1-inch (2.5-cm) pieces**
2	**red or green bell peppers, seeded and cut into 1-inch (2.5-cm) squares**
2	**medium red onions, quartered lengthwise and separated into layers**
12	**whole cherry tomatoes**
12	**medium metal or presoaked wooden skewers**

1 Combine all marinade ingredients in a non-reactive bowl. Add swordfish pieces and toss well to coat. Cover and marinate in the refrigerator for not more than 4 hours.

2 Drain marinade and reserve. Thread 4–5 pieces of swordfish onto each skewer, alternating with bell pepper and onion, and topped with a cherry tomato.

3 Grill over medium heat, turning and basting with reserved marinade frequently for 6–8 minutes.

4 Serve with fried or roasted potatoes, pita bread with *tzatziki* (recipe page 222) and salad, or rice pilaf.

LAMB and SAUSAGE skewers

Spiedini di Agnello e Salsiccia

These kebabs do not require any marinating and are popular fare in trattoria or family restaurants in and around Rome.

SERVES 6

1 lb • 500 g	spicy Italian sausages, cut into 1½-inch (4-cm) pieces
6 Tbsp • 90 mL	olive oil
2 Tbsp • 25 mL	red wine vinegar
1 lb • 500 g	boneless leg of lamb, cut into 1½-inch (4–cm) pieces
2	medium onions, quartered and layers separated
several	sage leaves
½ tsp • 2.5 mL	salt
½ tsp • 2.5 mL	freshly ground black pepper
12	medium metal or presoaked wooden skewers

1 Boil sausages in briskly boiling water for 3 minutes. Drain and set aside.

2 Combine olive oil and vinegar in a non-reactive bowl and set aside.

3 Thread lamb, onion, sausage and sage alternately onto skewers. Brush with oil and vinegar mixture and season with salt and pepper.

4 Grill on medium-high heat until lamb is slightly charred outside but pink inside, about 3–4 minutes per side. Turn and baste frequently with oil and vinegar mixture while grilling.

5 Serve with garlic bread and salad.

VEAL SKEWERS in marsala

Spiedini di vitello al Marsala

This preparation is unusual in that the meat is neither marinated nor grilled but sautéed in wine.

SERVES 8

2 lb • 1 kg	**boneless veal shoulder chops, cut into 1-inch (2.5-cm) cubes**
2	**medium onions, quartered and layers separated**
6 Tbsp • 90 mL	**olive oil**
1 tsp • 5 mL	**salt**
½ tsp • 2.5 mL	**freshly ground black pepper**
1 cup • 250 mL	**dry Marsala**
16	**short metal or wooden skewers**

1 Thread 3–4 veal cubes separated by onion layers onto each skewer.

2 Heat oil in shallow frying pan. When smoking, add skewers and brown meat on all sides. Season with salt and pepper.

3 Add wine to pan, turn heat up and boil until reduced by half. Cover, reduce heat and let skewers simmer for about 15 minutes, until meat is cooked and tender.

4 Serve immediately with risotto, polenta or salad.

SWORDFISH KEBABS

Spiedini di Pesce Spada

Swordfish kebabs are popular throughout Italy, particularly in the southern region bordering the Mediterranean and in Sicily.

SERVES 8

Marinade

½ cup • 125 mL	olive oil
¼ cup • 50 mL	lemon juice
1 Tbsp • 15 mL	lemon zest
2 tsp • 10 mL	minced garlic
1 tsp • 5 mL	chopped fresh flat-leaf parsley
1 tsp • 5 mL	chopped fresh oregano
1 tsp • 5 mL	chopped fresh marjoram
1 tsp • 5 mL	salt
½ tsp • 2.5 mL	freshly ground black pepper

Kebabs

2 lb • 1 kg	swordfish steaks, 1 inch (2.5 cm) thick, cut into 1½-inch (4-cm) pieces
2	lemons, cut in thin slices
4	medium tomatoes, each cut into 8 wedges
16	medium metal or presoaked bamboo skewers

1 In a non-reactive bowl, mix all marinade ingredients. Add swordfish pieces and toss gently. Cover and marinate for not more than 2 hours.

2 Drain marinade and reserve. Remove swordfish and thread 4–6 pieces with lemon slices in between them onto each skewer. Also thread 2 tomato wedges in between swordfish onto each skewer.

3 Grill over medium heat for about 10 minutes, turning and basting with reserved marinade frequently.

4 Serve with salad and lemon wedges.

LAMB KEBABS (SHASHLIK)   page 29

LAMB KEBABS (SOUVLAKI)   page 41

SWORDFISH KEBABS   page 48

LAMB SKEWERS WITH APRICOTS (SOSATIES)   page 98

SKEWERED MIXED GRILL
Spiedini di Carne Mista

This Sicilian preparation threads different cuts of meat onto two skewers.

SERVES 6

1 lb • 500 g	**Italian sausages**
1 lb • 500 g	**calves' liver, cut into 1½-inch (4-cm) long and ½-inch (1.2-cm) thick pieces**
1 lb • 500 g	**boneless chicken breasts, cut into 1½-inch (4-cm) cubes**
2 Tbsp • 25 mL	**olive oil**
	salt and black pepper to taste
½ cup • 125 mL	**breadcrumbs**
several	**sage leaves**
12	**medium metal or presoaked bamboo skewers**

1 Place sausages in a pan, cover with water and boil for 15–20 minutes. Drain and cut each sausage into 2-inch (5-cm) pieces. Slice each piece in half horizontally.

2 Sandwich each liver piece between 2 flat sides of split sausage. Thread 3 sausage sandwiches alternating with 2 chicken cubes and sage leaves onto 2 parallel skewers.

3 Brush with olive oil and season with salt and pepper; roll each skewer in breadcrumbs.

4 Grill skewers on medium heat for approximately 5–6 minutes per side.

5 Serve with fried potatoes or potato salad.

TURKEY KEBABS
Spiedini di Tacchino

SERVES 6

Marinade

¼ cup • 50 mL	olive oil
¼ cup • 50 mL	dry white wine
2 Tbsp • 25 mL	lemon juice
1 Tbsp • 15 mL	minced garlic
2 tsp • 10 mL	chopped fresh rosemary
2 tsp • 10 mL	chopped fresh flat-leaf parsley
2 tsp • 10 mL	chopped fresh sage
1 tsp • 5 mL	salt
½ tsp • 2.5 mL	freshly ground black pepper

Kebabs

2 lb • 1 kg	boneless turkey breasts cut into 1-inch (2.5-cm) cubes
2	narrow zucchini, cut crosswise into ¾-inch (2-cm) pieces
2	red bell peppers, seeded and cut into 1-inch (2.5-cm) squares
12	medium metal or presoaked bamboo skewers

1 In a large non-reactive bowl, combine marinade ingredients. Add cubed turkey and toss well to coat. Cover and marinate in the refrigerator overnight.

2 Drain marinade and reserve. Thread turkey alternating with zucchini and red pepper onto skewers. Brush with reserved marinade.

3 Grill over medium heat, turning and basting frequently with marinade, for about 10 minutes.

4 Serve with risotto, polenta or salad.

BEEF KEBABS

Spiedini di Bistecca

Marinade

SERVES 6

½ cup • 125 mL	olive oil
½ cup • 125 mL	red wine
¼ cup • 50 mL	red wine vinegar
1 Tbsp • 15 mL	lemon juice
1 tsp • 5 mL	dried oregano
1 tsp • 5 mL	dried thyme
1 tsp • 5 mL	salt
½ tsp • 2.5 mL	ground allspice
½ tsp • 2.5 mL	freshly ground black pepper

Kebabs

2 lb • 1 kg	rib-eye or top sirloin steak cut into 1-inch (2.5-cm) cubes
2	green bell peppers, seeded and cut into 1-inch (2.5-cm) squares
1	red onion, quartered, layers separated
12	medium metal skewers

1 Combine all marinade ingredients in a non-reactive bowl. Add beef pieces and toss well to coat. Cover and marinate in the refrigerator overnight.

2 Remove beef and reserve marinade. Thread beef cubes alternating with green pepper and onion onto each skewer. Let skewers rest for 15 minutes to reach room temperature.

3 Grill over high heat for about 4 minutes per side, turning and basting frequently with reserved marinade.

4 Serve with rice pilaf or risotto.

BEEF KEBABS

Szaszlyk Wolowy

These kebabs are not grilled over an open fire. Instead, they are fried in fat or oil.

SERVES 4

Marinade

3 Tbsp • 45 mL	**lemon juice**
1	**medium onion, finely chopped**
1 tsp • 5 mL	**salt**
½ tsp • 2.5 mL	**freshly ground black pepper**
½ tsp • 2.5 mL	**dried thyme**
½ tsp • 2.5 mL	**dried marjoram**

Kebabs

2 lb • 1 kg	**beef tenderloin or top sirloin steak, cut into 1½-inch (4-cm) pieces**
3	**bacon strips, cut into 1½-inch (4-cm) pieces**
1 Tbsp • 15 mL	**all-purpose flour**
8	**medium metal skewers**
2 Tbsp • 25 mL	**bacon fat or vegetable oil for frying**
1	**green onion, finely chopped**

1 Combine all marinade ingredients in a non-reactive bowl.

2 With a wooden mallet, pound beef pieces lightly to form flat discs.

3 Pour marinade over meat and toss well to coat thoroughly. Marinate overnight in the refrigerator.

4 Remove meat from marinade and sprinkle with flour. Thread about 5–6 pieces onto each skewer.

5 In a large frying pan heat fat or oil until smoking. Place skewers in pan and fry for about 5–6 minutes, turning constantly until all sides are brown and cooked. Remove and drain on paper towel.

6 Sprinkle with chopped green onion and serve with salad or rice.

LAMB KEBABS
Szaszlyk Barani

Marinade

2 Tbsp • 25 mL	olive oil
1 Tbsp • 15 mL	red wine vinegar
1	medium onion, finely chopped
1 tsp • 5 mL	salt
½ tsp • 2.5 mL	freshly ground black pepper

Kebabs

2 lb • 1 kg	boneless lamb (leg or shoulder), cut into 1½-inch (4-cm) pieces
3	bacon strips, cut into 1½-inch (4-cm) pieces
8	medium metal skewers
	butter for frying

1 Combine all marinade ingredients in a non-reactive bowl. Add lamb pieces and toss well to coat. Marinate for at least 4 hours.

2 Thread about 6 pieces of lamb alternating with bacon pieces onto each skewer.

3 Melt butter in a large frying pan and shallow fry skewers on medium-high heat, turning constantly so all sides are fully cooked, about 6–8 minutes.

4 Serve with rice or salad.

SKEWERED CHICKEN LIVER

Szaszlyki z Kurzych Watrobek

SERVES 4

1 lb • 500 g	chicken livers
2 cups • 500 mL	milk
½ tsp • 2.5 mL	salt
½ tsp • 2.5 mL	paprika
½ tsp • 2.5 mL	garlic powder
¼ tsp • 1.2 mL	nutmeg
2	bacon strips, cut into 1-inch (2.5-cm) pieces
8	short metal or bamboo skewers
	vegetable oil or butter for frying

1 Soak livers in milk for about half an hour. Drain, pat livers dry and set aside.

2 Combine salt, paprika, garlic powder and nutmeg. Sprinkle mixture over chicken livers.

3 Thread liver and bacon pieces alternately onto skewers.

4 In a frying pan heat vegetable oil or butter. Fry each skewer in hot oil for 2 minutes (or brush each skewer with oil or butter and grill over medium heat). Liver is done when brown on outside and pink inside.

5 Serve as an appetizer or as a main course with rice and a tomato, cucumber and onion salad.

SKEWERED BEEF

Espetada

This Portuguese specialty is popular in restaurants on the Island of Madeira where beef is grilled on special metal skewers with an eyelet on one end. Skewers are hung upside down on metal stands with bowls of fresh country bread, called pao, placed directly under the skewers to catch the meat juices and drippings.

Marinade

SERVES 4

¼ cup • 50 mL	olive oil
¼ cup • 50 mL	red wine vinegar
½ cup • 125 mL	flat-leaf parsley, chopped
1	medium onion, grated
6	bay leaves, crushed
1 Tbsp • 15 mL	minced garlic
1 tsp • 5 mL	salt
1 tsp • 5 mL	freshly ground black pepper

Kebabs

2 lb • 1 kg	beefsteak (tenderloin or top sirloin) cut into 1½-inch (4-m) cubes
8	medium metal skewers

1 Combine all marinade ingredients in a non-reactive bowl. Add beef and toss thoroughly to coat each piece. Cover and marinate overnight in the refrigerator.

2 Remove beef and reserve marinade. Thread 4–5 pieces onto each skewer. Let skewers rest for 20 minutes for beef to reach room temperature. Grill over high heat for about 4–5 minutes per side, turning frequently and basting with reserved marinade.

3 Serve the kebabs on or off the skewers over slices of Portuguese or French bread, and let the bread soak up the meat juices.

Spicy HOT SHRIMP KEBABS
Camaroes Grelhados Piri Piri

**SERVES 6
AS MAIN COURSE,
12 AS APPETIZER**

Marinade

½ cup • 125 mL	olive oil
2 Tbsp • 25 mL	lemon or lime juice
2 Tbsp • 25 mL	chopped fresh cilantro
2	red chilies, seeded and minced
1 Tbsp • 15 mL	minced garlic

Kebabs

| 2 lb • 1 kg | raw jumbo shrimps (16–20 count), peeled and deveined |
| 12 | medium presoaked bamboo skewers |

1 Combine marinade ingredients in a non-reactive bowl. Add shrimp and toss well to coat. Marinate in the refrigerator for not more than 2 hours.

2 Remove shrimp and reserve marinade. Thread 2–3 shrimps onto each skewer.

3 Grill over medium heat for about 2–3 minutes per side, turning often and basting with marinade.

3 Serve with little bowls of Molho de Piri Piri (hot red pepper sauce, see *piri piri*, page 230).

STURGEON KEBABS

Shashlik iz Osetrini

¼ cup • 50 mL	lemon juice
1 tsp • 5 mL	salt
½ tsp • 2.5 mL	freshly ground black pepper
2 lb • 1 kg	sturgeon steaks, cut into 1½-inch (4-cm) cubes
½ cup • 125 mL	sour cream
¼ cup • 50 mL	olive oil
8	medium metal skewers
(optional)	pomegranate sauce *(narsharab, page 230)*

1 Mix lemon juice with salt and pepper. Pour over sturgeon pieces, toss well, and marinate for about 30 minutes. In a separate bowl combine sour cream and olive oil.

2 Thread about 4–5 pieces of fish onto each skewer and brush liberally with sour cream/olive oil mixture.

3 Grill over medium-high heat for about 5 minutes per side, turning skewers and basting with sour cream/olive oil mixture occasionally.

4 Serve with green onion, tomato wedges, lemon slices and fresh cilantro leaves. For an added touch serve pomegranate sauce as a side dish (optional).

• *Sturgeon meat is firm and lends itself perfectly to grilling.*

• *These kebabs are a favorite in Russian restaurants.*

SPICY PORK KEBABS
Pinchitos Morunos

These Moorish-style kebabs are popular fare in tapas bars throughout Spain and especially so in the Andalusian region.

SERVES 8

Marinade

¼ cup • 50 mL	olive oil
2 Tbsp • 25 mL	lemon juice
2 Tbsp • 25 mL	chopped flat-leaf parsley
2 Tbsp • 25 mL	chopped cilantro leaves
2 tsp • 10 mL	garlic paste
2 tsp • 10 mL	curry powder
2 tsp • 10 mL	paprika
1 tsp • 5 mL	ground cumin
1 tsp • 5 mL	hot chili flakes or ½ teaspoon (2.5 mL) cayenne pepper
1 tsp • 5 mL	salt
1 tsp • 5 mL	freshly ground black pepper
½ tsp • 2.5 mL	dried thyme
½ tsp • 2.5 mL	dried oregano

Kebabs

2 lb • 1 kg	pork tenderloin, cut into 1-inch (2.5-cm) cubes
16	medium metal or presoaked wooden skewers
¼ cup • 50 mL	vegetable oil for basting

1 In a non-reactive bowl, combine all marinade ingredients. Add pork cubes and toss well to coat. Cover and marinate overnight in the refrigerator.

2 Remove pork pieces from marinade and thread 3–4 pieces onto each skewer. Grill over medium heat, turning and basting with oil frequently, for 8–10 minutes, or until outside of pork is crisp and inside no longer pink.

3 Serve as appetizers with potato or vegetable salad and lemon wedges.

LAMB KEBABS
Pinchos de Cordero

Marinade

½ cup • 125 mL	olive oil
2 Tbsp • 25 mL	lemon juice
¼ cup • 50 mL	chopped fresh rosemary
2 tsp • 10 mL	garlic paste
1 tsp • 5 mL	salt
½ tsp • 2.5 mL	freshly ground black pepper

Kebabs

2 lb • 1 kg	boneless leg of lamb, cut into 1-inch (2.5-cm) cubes
6	bacon strips, cut into 1-inch (2.5-cm) pieces
8	long metal skewers

1 In a non-reactive bowl, combine marinade ingredients. Add lamb pieces and toss well to coat. Cover and marinate up to 24 hours in the refrigerator.

2 Remove lamb and reserve marinade. Thread 6–8 lamb cubes alternating with bacon pieces onto each skewer. Let rest at room temperature for about 20 minutes before grilling.

3 Grill over medium-high heat for 8–10 minutes, turning frequently and basting with reserved marinade.

4 Serve with rice pilaf or salad.

FISH KEBABS

Pinchitos de Rape

Marinade

2 Tbsp • 25 mL	olive oil
2 Tbsp • 25 mL	lemon juice
1 Tbsp • 15 mL	minced garlic
1 tsp • 5 mL	ground cumin
1 tsp • 5 mL	salt
½ tsp • 2.5 mL	freshly ground black pepper

Kebabs

2 lb • 1 kg	fillet of monkfish or swordfish, cut into 1-inch (2.5-cm) pieces
2	green or red bell peppers, seeded and cut into 1-inch (2.5-cm) squares
12	medium presoaked wooden skewers
¼ cup • 50 mL	olive oil
¼ cup • 50 mL	dry sherry

1 In a non-reactive bowl, combine all marinade ingredients. Add fish pieces and toss well. Marinate for not more than 2 hours in the refrigerator.

2 Thread fish pieces alternately with bell pepper on the entire length of each skewer. Grill over medium heat until opaque, about 2–3 minutes per side, turning frequently, and basting with a mixture of olive oil and sherry.

3 Serve with salad and lemon wedges.

LAMB KEBABS

Shashlyk

Marinade

½ cup • 125 mL	olive oil
½ cup • 125 mL	dry red wine
¼ cup • 50 mL	vinegar
1	large onion, finely chopped
3 Tbsp • 45 mL	freshly grated horseradish
1 tsp • 5 mL	garlic paste
2	bay leaves, crushed
1 tsp • 5 mL	salt
1 tsp • 5 mL	sugar
½ tsp • 2.5 mL	freshly ground black pepper
½ tsp • 2.5 mL	dried marjoram

Kebabs

2 lb • 1 kg	boneless leg of lamb, excess fat removed and cut into 1½-inch (4-cm) pieces
8	medium metal skewers

1 Combine all marinade ingredients in a non-reactive bowl. Add lamb pieces and toss well to coat. Cover and marinate in the refrigerator overnight.

2 Drain marinade and reserve. Thread 5–6 lamb pieces onto each skewer. Brush generously with marinade.

3 Grill skewers over medium-high heat for about 10–12 minutes, turning and basting with reserved marinade occasionally.

4 Serve over a bed of hot rice.

Ground MEAT KEBABS

Cevapcici

SERVES 8

1 lb • 500 g	**ground beef**
½ lb • 250 g	**ground lamb**
½ lb • 250 g	**ground pork**
1	**large onion, finely chopped**
1 Tbsp • 15 mL	**paprika**
1 tsp • 5 mL	**freshly ground black pepper**
1 tsp • 5 mL	**garlic paste**
1½ tsp • 7.5 mL	**salt**
½ tsp • 2.5 mL	**cayenne pepper**
1	**egg, lightly beaten**
	melted lard or olive oil for basting
8	**long metal skewers**

1. In a large bowl, mix ground meats with onion, paprika, black pepper, garlic, salt, cayenne pepper and egg. Knead well with hands, cover and refrigerate overnight to allow flavors to develop.

2. Shape into cylinders, about 2 inches (5 cm) long and 1 inch (2.5 cm) in diameter, around skewers, about 4 cylinders per skewer. Brush with lard or oil.

3. Grill skewers over high heat, turning and basting frequently, until brown on all sides.

4. Serve with chopped onions and yogurt-cucumber sauce.

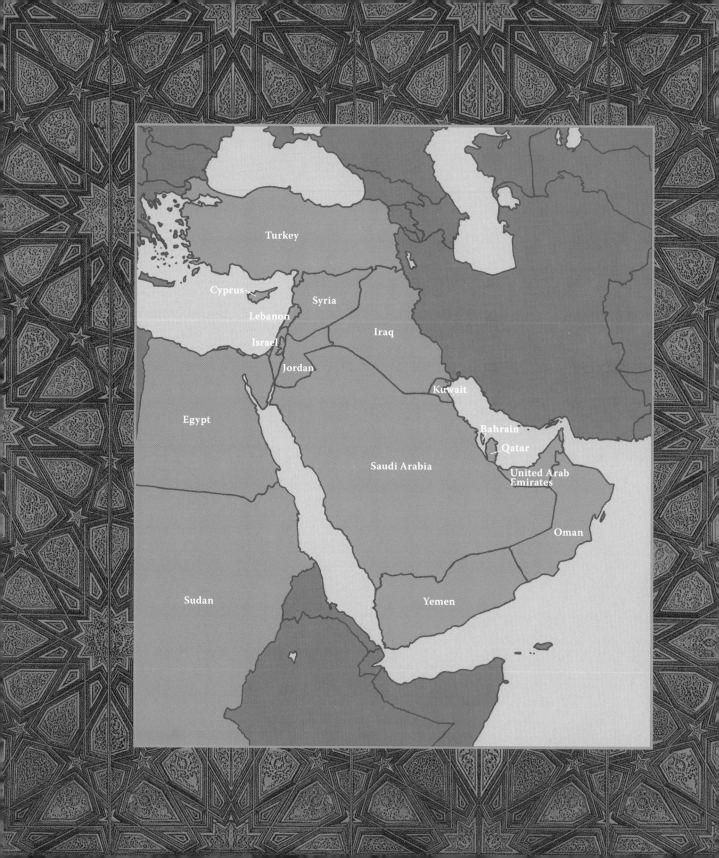

The Middle East

There is no consensus as to which countries constitute the Middle East, but this region is essentially where Africa, Asia and Europe meet. Some argue that predominantly Muslim countries of North Africa, like Morocco, Algeria, Tunisia and Libya, be recognized as Middle Eastern countries, whereas others see them as too geographically remote to be identified as truly Middle Eastern. Countries traditionally considered part of the Middle East include Syria, Jordan, Lebanon, Israel, Egypt, Sudan, Iraq, Kuwait, Saudi Arabia, Qatar, the United Arab Emirates, Bahrain, Yemen and Oman. Most of these countries are Arabic-speaking, predominantly Muslim and have similar culinary and cultural affinities and characteristics. Turkey, which straddles Europe and Asia, is included as part of the Middle East because of its deep roots in the Arab-Islamic world.

Middle Eastern cookery has evolved over many centuries and has incorporated culinary contributions and traits from various colonizers, migrants, traders and indigenous inhabitants. Modern Middle Eastern cuisine is a synthesis of influences from Turkey, Persia and Asia. In Middle Eastern cooking the use of herbs is extensive and varies from country to country. Typical seasonings used in kebab cookery might include mint, flat-leaf parsley, basil, garlic, lemon, olive oil, onion juice, coriander, cumin, cloves, cinnamon and chilies. Traditional kebab meat is goat, mutton or lamb; other meats, like beef, veal, chicken, duck and fish, are also used but never pork because of religious taboos.

Although kebabs are common street food throughout the Middle East, in the Gulf States of Kuwait, Saudi Arabia, the United Arab Emirates, Qatar, Oman and Bahrain they are particularly popular. Skewered succulent pieces of juicy tender lamb *(laham mashwi)* or seasoned ground lamb *(kabab mashwi)* wrapped around flat skewers and grilled over hot coals are common fare in many restaurants and food stalls throughout the Gulf States. These kebabs, referred to as Gulf hamburgers, are usually served inside Arabian flatbread called *khoubiz* (see page 229) with tomato and cucumber slices, shredded lettuce and a sprinkling of *sumac* powder (see page 233).

Seasoned ground-meat kebabs are favored in roadside restaurants and open-air food stalls all across Egypt, Jordan, Syria, Iraq, Kuwait and Lebanon. In Egypt they are known as *kofta meshweya* or *kofta alla shish* and are a common street food. In Lebanon, where they are called *kaftah* or *kufta meshwiyeh*, street vendors wrap a pita bread around the cooked kebabs, to soak up the cooking juices and pull the meat off the skewer. The spicier version of ground meat kebabs, called *kiymeh mashwi Omani*, is found in Oman. Without any doubt it owes its origin to India because the term *kiymeh* is derived from the Indian word *qeema* or *kheema* for ground meat, and many Indian spices are used in its preparation.

Turkey is where kebab culture evolved over centuries. It spread to neighboring countries and beyond during the reign of the Ottoman Empire and continues to flourish today. Turkish cuisine is said to be highly influenced by Persian cuisine and this is particularly evident in the development of kebab cookery. Although the word *kabab* is of Persian origin and describes all kinds of grilled meats, historical records indicate that the Turks were well acquainted with the art of grilling meats and had developed many more varieties of kebab forms than their Persian colonizers had.

Kebabs are Turkey's fast food, but venues range from modest street vendors to well-established kebab houses to elegant restaurants where a variety of skewered delicacies are offered as a snack or a full meal. In larger cities like Istanbul, Izmir and Ankara, kebab shops or kebab houses, known as *kebapci* or *ocakbasi*, are popular outlets for an inexpensive but satisfying meal. A variety of kebabs are attractively and elegantly displayed in show windows or glass cases outside their entrances and customers are drawn by the tantalizing aroma of grilled meat and

fat dripping on a wood fire. Other informal, inexpensive, no-frills eateries specialize in grilled or broiled ground lamb meatballs threaded onto skewers and called *kofteci*. The Turkish State of Anatolia is famous for its *kebapci*, but the greatest variety of kebabs is found in the southeastern part of Turkey, where the kebabs tend to be spicier.

As a rule, Turks use spices rather sparingly in their kebab preparation in order not to mask the natural flavor and taste of the grilled meat. Predominant herbs and spices in cooking include parsley, mint, dill, bay leaves, pepper, allspice, cinnamon, paprika and chili flakes. Lamb is the most common meat for kebabs, although beef and chicken are increasingly available in large cities. The most popular street food is probably *kofte* or *sis kofte* made with finely minced lamb mixed with lamb fat and seasoning, wrapped around a flat metal skewer for grilling.

Probably the preferred street food in Turkey is *doner kebap*, which consists of thin slices of meat (mostly lamb or chicken but sometimes beef) with layers of fat stacked on a vertical spit and grilled slowly while rotating between heat sources. Slightly charred cooked meat is shaved off in thin slices and served either inside a pita pocket or on top of a Turkish *pide* bread with salad ingredients. Doner kebabs are a favorite lunchtime treat, whereas other kebabs are preferred in the evening. In Greece doner kebabs are called *gyros*, in Lebanon and other Arabic-speaking countries they are referred to as *shwarma* or *shawarma*. Turkish doner kebabs have become a ubiquitous fast food across Europe, and numerous small eateries selling these kebabs are also popular gathering places that provide a social oasis for Turkish expatriates.

- *Several varieties of kebabs in the Turkish culinary repertoire are enjoyed by visitors and natives alike. The popular* adana kebap, *named after the city of Adana, made from spiced ground lamb, and its non-spicy variant the* urfa kebap, *along with* sis kebap *(skewered cubes of lamb alternating with pepper and onion),* kofte kebap *(ground lamb mixed with rice, bulgar or bread crumbs),* patlicanli kebap *(ground lamb patties between pieces of eggplant),* domatesi kebap *(tomato and ground lamb),* kesarli kebap *(mixed grill) and* tavuk sis *(chicken kebob) are mainstays of a well-established Turkish kebab house.*

SKEWERED SAUSAGES

Sheftalia or Sausenges

SERVES 4–8

1 lb • 500 g	**finely ground fatty pork**
1 lb • 500 g	**finely ground lamb or veal**
1	**large onion, finely chopped**
½ cup • 125 mL	**finely chopped flat-leaf parsley**
2 tsp • 10 mL	**salt**
1 tsp • 5 mL	**freshly ground black pepper**
½ lb • 250 g	**pig fat strips (*panna*), or bacon strips cut into 4-inch (10-cm) squares**
8	**long flat narrow metal skewers**

1 Mix together ground meats, onion, parsley, salt and pepper. Knead well with hands to form a firm consistency. If not very firm, place in the refrigerator for a few hours.

2 Wet hands and shape meat mixture into small sausages, 2 inches (5 cm) long and ½–1 inch (1.5–2.5 cm) wide. Roll each sausage inside a *panna* or bacon strip.

3 Thread 4 wrapped sausages onto each skewer, leaving a space between them. Grill over medium heat, turning the skewers frequently. The skewers require slow cooking to ensure the inside is well cooked.

4 When nicely browned on all sides, remove skewers from heat. Serve either as an appetizer or a main course.

• *The* panna *or bacon fat will melt during grilling, keeping the sausage meat moist and also imparting a nice flavor. These sausages are a delicacy on the island of Cyprus.*

SKEWERED LAMB

Lahma Mashwiya

Marinade

2	grated onions
2 Tbsp • 25 mL	lime juice
1 tsp • 5 mL	salt
1 tsp • 5 mL	freshly ground black pepper

Kebabs

2 lb • 1 kg	boneless lamb leg , cut into 1¼-inch (3-cm) cubes
½ lb • 125 g	lamb fat, cut into 1-inch (2.5-cm) pieces
8	long narrow flat metal skewers
2 Tbsp • 25 mL	chopped fresh parsley

1 Combine all marinade ingredients in a bowl. Add lamb and toss well. Cover and marinate in the refrigerator overnight and up to 24 hours.

2 Thread 6–8 pieces of lamb alternating with lamb fat onto each skewer.

3 Grill over medium-high heat, turning frequently, until the meat is brown on the outside and pink inside, about 10 minutes.

4 Sprinkle with chopped parsley and serve with Egyptian bread (*eeish baladi*, page 228) or pita bread and salad.

MEAT and EGGPLANT kebabs
Laham Qasma Mishwee

SERVES 6

Marinade

¼ cup • 50 mL	olive oil
¼ cup • 50 mL	lemon juice
1 tsp • 5 mL	salt
1 tsp • 5 mL	ground allspice
½ tsp • 2.5 mL	freshly ground black pepper

Kebabs

2 lb • 1 kg	boneless lamb leg or lean beef, cut into 1-inch (2.5-cm) cubes
1	large eggplant, cut into 1-inch (2.5-cm) cubes
1	medium onion, quartered and layers separated
2	green bell peppers, seeded and cut into 1-inch (2.5-cm) squares
2 cups • 500 mL	tomato juice
12	medium metal skewers

1 Combine all marinade ingredients in a large non-reactive bowl. Add meat and eggplant pieces. Toss gently, cover and marinate in the refrigerator for up to 4 hours.

2 Remove meat and eggplant from marinade. Thread meat, alternating with eggplant, onion and green pepper, onto each skewer.

3 Grill over high heat, about 2 minutes per side. Remove skewers and place in a wide frying pan. Add tomato juice, cover and simmer over low heat for 10–15 minutes or until skewers are fully cooked.

4 Serve over rice.

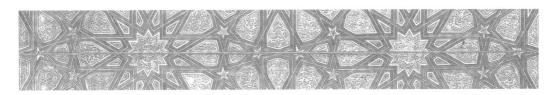

CHICKEN KEBABS

Shish Tauok

Marinade

½ cup • 125 mL	**lemon juice**
1	**medium onion, grated**
2 Tbsp • 25 mL	**olive oil**
1 Tbsp • 15 mL	**chopped fresh mint**
1 tsp • 5 mL	**ground anise seeds**
1 tsp • 5 mL	**salt**
½ tsp • 2.5 mL	**freshly ground black pepper**

Kebabs

2 lb • 1 kg	**boneless, skinless chicken breasts cut into 1½-inch (4-cm) cubes**
1	**red onion, quartered and layers separated**
1	**red bell pepper, seeded and cut into 1½-inch (4-cm) squares**
1	**green bell pepper, seeded and cut into 1½-inch (4-cm) squares**
8	**long metal skewers**

1 Combine all marinade ingredients in a non-metallic bowl. Add chicken cubes and toss well to coat thoroughly. Cover and marinate in the refrigerator for at least 2 hours and preferably overnight.

2 Drain marinade and reserve. Thread chicken pieces, alternating with onion and red and green peppers onto each skewer.

3 Grill over medium heat, basting once with reserved marinade, for about 3–4 minutes per side.

4 Serve with pita bread and salad.

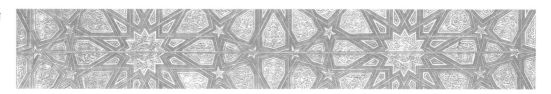

LAMB KEBABS

Lahem Meshwi

SERVES 4

Marinade

2 Tbsp • 25 mL	lemon juice
2 Tbsp • 25 mL	olive oil
1 Tbsp • 15 mL	minced garlic
1 tsp • 5 mL	salt
½ tsp • 2.5 mL	ground allspice
½ tsp • 2.5 mL	ground cinnamon
½ tsp • 2.5 mL	freshly ground black pepper

Kebabs

2 lb • 1 kg	boneless leg of lamb, excess fat removed, cut into 1½-inch (4-cm) pieces
2	medium onions, quartered and layers separated
8	long metal skewers
	olive oil for basting

1 Combine all marinade ingredients in a non-reactive bowl. Add lamb and toss well. Cover and marinate for at least 2 hours at room temperature, but preferably overnight in the refrigerator.

2 Remove lamb from marinade, reserving marinade. Thread 5–6 pieces of lamb, alternating with onion onto each skewer.

3 Grill over medium-high heat, turning and basting with reserved marinade, for about 4 minutes per side. Brush with olive oil toward the end of cooking.

4 Serve with rice pilaf.

LIVER KEBABS

Mi'laag Mashwi bi Toum

SERVES 4

1 lb • 500 g	lamb or goat liver
1 tsp • 5 mL	garlic paste
½ tsp • 2.5 mL	dried mint
¼ cup • 50 mL	olive oil
½ tsp • 2.5 mL	salt
½ tsp • 2.5 mL	freshly ground black pepper
8	medium metal or presoaked bamboo skewers
	lemon wedges for garnish

1 Soak liver in cold salted water for 30 minutes. Drain, pat dry and remove outer membrane. Cut into 1-inch (2.5-cm) squares.

2 Combine garlic paste with mint and spread over liver pieces. Sprinkle with olive oil, salt and black pepper. Toss well, cover and marinate for an hour.

3 Remove liver and reserve marinade. Thread liver pieces onto skewers.

4 Grill over medium-high heat, about 2 minutes per side. Brush with reserved marinade.

5 Serve as an appetizer, garnished with lemon wedges.

LAMB KEBABS

Kabab Halabi

SERVES 6

Marinade

2	**medium onions, grated**
1 Tbsp • 15 mL	**paprika**
1 tsp • 5 mL	**salt**
½ tsp • 2.5 mL	**freshly ground black pepper**

Kebabs

2 lb • 1 kg	**boneless leg of lamb, cut into 1-inch (2.5-cm) cubes**
12	**medium metal skewers**
2 Tbsp • 25 mL	**olive oil**
2	**large tomatoes, chopped**
3	**pita breads**

1 Combine marinade ingredients in a bowl. Add lamb and toss well. Cover and marinate in the refrigerator for at least 4 hours, preferably overnight.

2 Strain and reserve marinade. Thread 4–5 pieces of lamb onto each skewer and set aside.

3 Prepare a sauce by heating olive oil in a pan and adding chopped tomatoes and strained marinade. Bring mixture to a boil, reduce heat, cover and let simmer for 5 minutes or more until a smooth paste is formed.

4 Grill skewers over medium-high heat, turning often, for 8–10 minutes.

5 Cut pita bread into ½-inch (1-cm) strips, and place on a serving plate. Slide meat off skewers over bread strips, pour sauce over kebabs and serve.

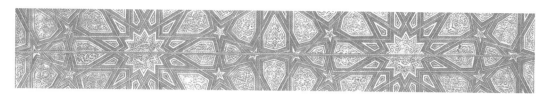

Ground MEAT KEBABS

Kufta Mishwiya

SERVES 8

2 lb • 1 kg	**finely ground lamb or lean beef**
2	**medium onions, grated**
½ cup • 125 mL	**finely chopped flat-leaf parsley**
1 tsp • 5 mL	**ground allspice**
1 tsp • 5 mL	**dried mint**
1 tsp • 5 mL	**salt**
½ tsp • 2.5 mL	**freshly ground black pepper**
½ tsp • 2.5 mL	**cayenne pepper**
½ tsp • 2.5 mL	**ground cinnamon**
8	**long, narrow, flat metal skewers**

1 Mix ground meat with onion, parsley, allspice, mint, salt, peppers and cinnamon in a large non-reactive bowl. Knead with hands to ensure meat is thoroughly mixed with herbs and spices. Cover and refrigerate for at least 4 hours, preferably overnight, to develop flavors.

2 Divide meat mixture into 8 portions. Wet hands and form long, sausage-like shape at least 1 inch (2.5 cm) in diameter around each skewer.

3 Suspend skewers directly over hot fire (remove the cooking grill), using the edges of the fire box to support the ends of the skewers. Turn skewers frequently until the meat is cooked and evenly brown on all sides, about 6–8 minutes.

4 Slide cooked kebabs off skewers and serve with salad and pita bread.

Ground LAMB KEBABS
Kabab Mashwi

SERVES 8

2 lb • 1 kg	**double-ground lamb**
2	**large onions, grated**
1 cup • 250 mL	**chopped flat-leaf parsley**
1½ tsp • 7.5 mL	**salt**
2 tsp • 10 mL	***baharat* (page 228)**
16	**long flat metal skewers**
¼ cup • 50 mL	**vegetable oil for basting**

1 Mix ground lamb with onion, parsley, salt and *baharat*. Knead with hands to form a smooth, firm mixture. Cover and refrigerate for at least 2 hours to allow flavors to develop.

2 Divide mixture into 16 portions. Moisten hands with water and mold each portion around a skewer to form a sausage-like shape 4–6 inches (10–15 cm) long. Place the skewers across a pan with edges so the kebabs do not touch the bottom and hang freely.

3 Brush kebabs with oil and suspend skewers directly over the fire box (remove the cooking grill) using the edges of the fire box to support the skewers. Grill about 3 minutes per side.

4 Remove kebabs from skewers and serve in warmed *khoubiz* bread (page 229), with salad or over rice or bulgar.

• *These kebabs are popular throughout Saudi Arabia, Kuwait, the United Arab Emirates, Bahrain, Qatar and Oman. They are generally served in warmed flat bread called* khoubiz.

Spicy MINCED LAMB KEBABS
Adana Kebap

SERVES 4

1 lb • 500 g	**double-ground lamb**
¼ cup • 50 mL	**lamb fat or butter**
1 cup • 250 mL	**finely grated onion**
½ cup • 125 mL	**finely chopped flat-leaf parsley**
2 tsp • 10 mL	**garlic paste**
1 tsp • 5 mL	**red pepper flakes**
1 tsp • 5 mL	**cayenne pepper**
½ tsp • 2.5 mL	**salt**
½ tsp • 2.5 mL	**freshly ground black pepper**
8	**long, flat metal skewers**
	vegetable oil or melted butter for basting
	sumac (page 233) for sprinkling

1 Mix ground lamb, fat, onion, parsley, garlic, all peppers and salt by hand to form a firm mixture. Cover and refrigerate overnight.

2 Divide lamb mixture into 8 portions. Wet hands and mold each portion around a skewer to form a 6–8 inch (15–20 cm) sausage. Press meat onto skewer at intervals to ensure adherence.

3 Grill over hot fire, about 2–3 minutes per side, basting with oil or butter.

4 Serve over *pide* bread (page 230) with sliced onion and tomato. Sprinkle with sumac.

• *Turks prefer lamb fat which is easily available and imparts a special flavor to Adana kebabs. Turkish kebabs are usually served with a buttered and toasted piece of flat bread called* pide *accompanied by a variety of colorful salad ingredients such as grated carrots, sliced red cabbage, chopped green salad, slices of red onion, tomato wedges and even steamed rice, all sprinkled with sumac.*

CHICKEN KEBABS

Tavuk Sis

SERVES 4

Marinade

⅓ cup • 75 mL	olive oil
⅓ cup • 75 mL	lemon juice
2 tsp • 10 mL	dried thyme
1 tsp • 5 mL	minced garlic
1 tsp • 5 mL	salt
½ tsp • 2.5 mL	freshly ground black pepper

Kebabs

4	boneless chicken breasts or 8 boneless thighs, cut into 1-inch (2.5-cm) cubes
1	medium red onion, quartered and layers separated
2	green bell peppers, seeded and cut into 1-inch (2.5-cm) squares
3	medium tomatoes, each cut into 8 wedges
8	medium metal or presoaked bamboo skewers

1 Combine all marinade ingredients in a non-reactive bowl. Add chicken and toss well to coat. Cover and marinate in the refrigerator for at least 4 hours or preferably overnight.

2 Drain marinade and reserve. Thread 4–5 chicken cubes alternating with onion, green pepper and tomato onto each skewer.

3 Grill skewers over medium heat for 7–10 minutes, turning and basting with reserved marinade frequently.

4 Serve with rice pilaf or mixed salad.

SKEWERED SWORDFISH

Kilic Baligi Siste or Kilic Sis

Marinade

SERVES 6

⅓ cup • 75 mL	olive oil
⅓ cup • 75 mL	lemon juice
¼ cup • 50 mL	onion juice (1 grated onion, squeezed)
2	bay leaves, crumbled
1 tsp • 5 mL	paprika
1 tsp • 5 mL	salt
½ tsp • 2.5 mL	freshly ground black pepper
½ tsp • 2.5 mL	red pepper flakes

Kebabs

2 lb • 1 kg	swordfish steaks, 1 inch (2.5 cm) thick, cut into 1¼-inch (3-cm) pieces
1	medium red onion, quartered and layers separated
2	green or red bell peppers, seeded and cut into 1½-inch (4-cm) squares
3	medium tomatoes, each cut into 8 wedges
1	large lemon, cut into slices
several	bay leaves
12	long metal skewers

1 Combine all marinade ingredients in a non-reactive bowl. Add fish pieces and toss well to coat thoroughly. Marinate for 3–4 hours in the refrigerator.

2 Drain marinade and reserve. Thread fish alternating with onion, bell pepper, tomato, lemon slice and bay leaf onto each skewer.

3 Grill over medium heat, 5 minutes per side, turning and basting with reserved marinade frequently.

4 Serve with lemon sauce over rice pilaf or crusty bread and salad.

• *Swordfish kebabs are sold in numerous fish eateries along the Turkish Aegean. Several fish stalls under the famous Galata Bridge in Istanbul specialize in skewered swordfish served with lemon sauce (limon salcasi). Turkish lemon sauce is available in stores specializing in Middle Eastern food, or can be made at home by combining ¼ cup (50 mL) each of lemon juice, extra virgin olive oil and chopped fresh parsley, with freshly ground black pepper to taste.*

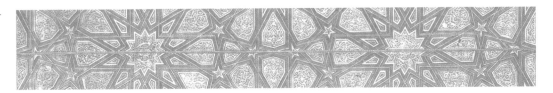

LAMB KEBABS with yogurt
Yogurtlu Kebap

SERVES 4

Marinade

2 Tbsp • 25 mL	olive oil
2 Tbsp • 25 mL	lemon juice
1	medium onion, grated
1 tsp • 5 mL	ground cumin
1 tsp • 5 mL	garlic paste
1 tsp • 5 mL	paprika
1 tsp • 5 mL	salt
½ tsp • 2.5 mL	freshly ground pepper
½ tsp • 2.5 mL	dried thyme
½ tsp • 2.5 mL	dried oregano

Kebabs

2 lb • 1 kg	boneless lamb (leg or shoulder), cut into 1-inch (2.5-cm) cubes
8	medium metal skewers
½ cup • 125 mL	tomato sauce
2	*pide* (page 230), each cut into 4 pieces
½ cup • 125 mL	beaten yogurt
¼ cup • 50 mL	chopped fresh parsley
2 Tbsp • 25 mL	pine nuts
	sumac (page 233) for sprinkling

1 Mix all marinade ingredients in a bowl. Add lamb, toss well to coat, cover and marinate for up to 24 hours in the refrigerator.

2 Drain marinade and reserve. Thread 6–8 pieces of lamb onto each skewer leaving ¼ inch (0.5 cm) space between pieces.

3 Grill over medium-high heat for about 4–5 minutes per side, basting with reserved marinade occasionally.

4 Toast *pide* briefly on the grill and spread with warmed tomato sauce. Serve kebabs on the bread and pour yogurt over kebabs. Sprinkle with chopped parsley, pine nuts and sumac.

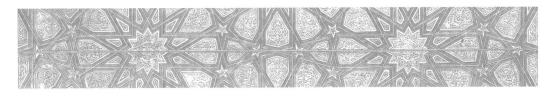

WRAPPED ground MEAT kebabs
Beyti Kebap

SERVES 8

2 lb • 1 kg	**ground lamb or beef**
½ cup • 125 mL	**finely chopped flat-leaf parsley**
2	**medium onions, grated**
1 tsp • 5 mL	**garlic paste**
1 tsp • 5 mL	**red pepper flakes**
1 tsp • 5 mL	**ground cumin**
1 tsp • 5 mL	**salt**
1 tsp • 5 mL	**freshly ground black pepper**
8	**long, narrow, flat metal skewers** *lavash* **bread (see page 229) for wrapping**

1 Mix ground meat with parsley, onion, garlic, red pepper, cumin, salt and pepper. Knead the mixture to form a firm dough. Let rest in the refrigerator overnight to develop the flavors.

2 Divide meat mixture into 8 portions. Wet hands and wrap each portion around a skewer and form a sausage about 6–8 inches (15–20 cm) long.

3 Suspend skewers directly over hot fire (remove the cooking grill), using the edges of the fire box to support ends of skewers. Turn skewers frequently until meat is evenly cooked on all sides, about 4–6 minutes.

4 Remove skewers from grill and wrap each kebab in *lavash* bread. Grill each skewer again for about 2 minutes, turning constantly to ensure kebabs are moist and fully cooked and *lavash* is slightly toasted.

5 Remove each wrapped kebab from the skewer, cut across into 2-inch (5-cm) rolls and serve with yogurt-garlic sauce.

LAMB KEBABS

Sis Kebap

SERVES 4

Marinade

½ cup • 125 mL	onion juice (2 grated onions, squeezed)
¼ cup • 50 mL	olive oil
2 Tbsp • 25 mL	lemon juice
1 tsp • 5 mL	garlic paste
1 tsp • 5 mL	salt
½ tsp • 2.5 mL	dried thyme
½ tsp • 2.5 mL	freshly ground black pepper
2	bay leaves, crushed

Kebabs

2 lb • 1 kg	boneless lamb (leg or shoulder), cut into 1¼-inch (3-cm) cubes
1	medium red onion, quartered and layers separated
1	red bell pepper, cut into 1½-inch (4-cm) squares
1	green bell pepper, cut into 1½-inch (4-cm) squares
8	long metal skewers
	chopped fresh parsley and sumac for sprinkling

1 Mix all marinade ingredients in a non-reactive bowl. Add lamb and toss well to coat thoroughly. Cover and marinate in the refrigerator for up to 24 hours.

2 Drain marinade and reserve. Thread 5–6 pieces of lamb alternating with onion and bell peppers onto each skewer.

3 Grill over medium-high heat for 10-12 minutes, turning and basting frequently with reserved marinade.

4 Serve over rice pilaf or *pide* (see page 230). Sprinkle with chopped parsley and sumac.

Africa

Africa is recognized as a continent of diversity, not only of languages, ethnic origins, cultures and climate, but also of cuisines. It is often said that the linguistic diversity of the African continent far exceeds its culinary diversity, implying that a food item may have many different names depending on the area. In sub-Saharan Africa, where hundreds of languages are spoken, it is difficult, if not impossible, to associate an indigenous cuisine with a particular country. But it can be said that most Africans in this region have no easy access to fresh meat, fish or poultry and supplement their diet mainly with legumes, cassava and vegetables such as yams, corn and squash. Perhaps because of this, soups, stews and curries are common throughout Africa. Where it is available, mutton is the preferred meat, followed by beef.

The kebab culture is not widespread in Africa and is generally confined to coastal areas. North African countries bordering the Mediterranean from Morocco in the west to Egypt in the east are predominantly Islamic, and Muslim dietary rules generally prevail. These countries have little in common either culturally or gastronomically with the rest of Africa. North African cuisine has developed over centuries through the influence of invaders, traders, settlers and visitors from other parts of Africa, the Middle East and Europe. Morocco, Tunisia, Algeria and sometimes Libya represent the North African group of countries collectively referred to by historians as the Maghreb, meaning "the west" or "the land of the setting sun." The cuisines of these countries are characterized by the intense cultural interaction that occurred not only with the Phoenicians, nomadic Berbers, Romans, Turks and Arabs in ancient times, but also, in recent times, with other European countries bordering the Mediterranean such as Spain, France and Italy.

In Morocco, kebab culture is firmly established and kebabs are a common street food available almost everywhere. Marrakech, well known to tourists, can be regarded as the kebab capital of Morocco. The famous town square of Djemaa el-Fna during daylight hours is a colorful throbbing marketplace complete with acrobats, snake charmers, story tellers, fortune tellers, musicians and dancers. But as night falls, the square is transformed into a giant food court where rows of stalls lit by hurricane lanterns serve all kinds of local delicacies. A smoky haze envelops the square from a multitude of food vendors and "brochetteries" grilling a variety of

Moroccan kebabs and filling the air with their tantalizing aroma.

Lamb is used most often for kebabs in Morocco, but there are beef, chicken and even camel hump kebabs. The meat is generally coated with a mixture of dry spices, which ensures a crispy texture, or marinated in herbs, spices, lemon juice and olive oil. The practice of alternating suet with meat enhances the flavor and moisture of the kebabs. Commonly used flavorings include cumin, cinnamon, cloves, black pepper, paprika, ginger, garlic, grated onion, parsley, cilantro and lemon rind. Kebabs are served on the street with the traditional *ksra* bread; it is half opened and kebabs hot off the grill are slipped into its pocket, along with all the juices and drippings, and it is then eaten like a sandwich. A hot sauce called *harissa* (recipe page 224) and a dry mixture of ground cumin and salt is usually served with the kebabs.

Tunisian food is characterized by its fiery hot seasonings, and harissa is the mainstay of many Tunisian dishes. Lamb is the first choice for meat but beef is also used. A long coastline ensures a good supply of fresh fish and seafood. Spicy lamb kebabs grilled with tomatoes, peppers and onion, called *mechoui*—in French, *brochettes d'agneau*—are popular street food. Tunisians generally sprinkle a spice mixture called *tabil* (see page 231) over their kebabs and grilled meats.

Algerian cuisine is midway between highly aromatic Moroccan food and fiery-hot Tunisian food. Common spices and herbs include cumin, cinnamon, coriander, allspice and pepper. Lamb or mutton is the most common meat as it is difficult to raise other farm animals in the semi-arid conditions that prevail in most of the country. Algeria was a French colony for over a century, and the French influence is well entrenched. Street vendors and food stalls everywhere sell lamb kebabs, or brochettes as they are commonly known, tucked into a French loaf with a spicy sauce. French Algerians prefer brochettes of lamb organ meats, such as sweetbread, kidney, liver, or heart. Lamb kefta or spiced meatball kebabs are also sold by street vendors. Libyan cuisine is a mixture of Arabic, Mediterranean and Italian influences. Mutton, chicken and swordfish kebabs are popular street food.

Throughout the countries of West Africa (Benin, Gambia, Ghana, Guinea, Liberia, Mali, Nigeria, Senegal, Sierra Leone and the Ivory Coast), street vendors selling skewers of grilled meat are a common sight. Generally speaking, the cuisines of these countries can be regarded as truly indigenous because the European powers that colonized these lands had little or no influence on the local cuisine. West African food is highly seasoned and chilies and ground peanuts play an important role.

Nigerians in particular like their food fiery-hot. In Nigeria mutton (goat meat) is commonly used and beef and poultry are widely accepted; pork is less common because a significant number of Nigerians are Muslim. Spicy beef kebabs called *suya* or *tsire* are a national fast food in Nigeria. They are as ubiquitous as hot dogs in North America and are popular street food in countries outside Nigeria as well. Beef is the most common meat for *suya* but chicken and veal laced with cayenne pepper and ground peanuts are also used.

In East Africa, the inland cuisine is very much indigenous African, but the coastal cuisine shows heavy Middle Eastern and Indian influences, partly due to brisk trade between East African ports and the Middle East and India and partly because significant numbers of Arabs and Indians settled here. Indian cuisine introduced by migrants who settled in Kenya, Uganda and Tanzania had a profound impact on the local cuisine. Most of the kebabs available here have a noticeable Indian character from the use of spices and herbs such as cumin, coriander, ginger, chili, cinnamon, cloves, garlic and cilantro. Kofta kebabs, sold on the street in Mombasa and made of ground lamb and spices, are no different from those found in India and were first introduced in Kenya by Indian traders and businessmen. The multi-ethnic island of Zanzibar on the coast of Tanzania is known for its Swahili shish kebab called *mishkaki*, which uses chicken or beef marinated in Indian spices.

South African cuisine reflects a blending of African, Middle Eastern, Indian, Malaysian and European culinary cultures. In the 16th century, the Boers imported slaves from Dutch colonies in what is now Indonesia to work on their land. The men worked on the farms and elsewhere, and the women were assigned tasks like cooking and cleaning. The slaves used spices to liven up the otherwise insipid Dutch food and their descendents, known as Cape Malay, subsequently developed a hybrid of Dutch, English and Malay food known as the Old Cape cookery. This, combined with the influence of migrants from India who came to work on sugar cane farms and build the South African railways, had a considerable impact on South African cuisine, and foods like curries, *sambals* (blend of hot chilies and seasonings), *atjar* (pickles and relishes) and chutneys have now become an integral part of its cuisine. Today Cape Malay food is common in the urban centers of South Africa and one of the most popular items is *sosaties*—South African kebabs with Malay seasoning and the name "*sosaties*" is derived from the Malay word *sate* for grilled meat.

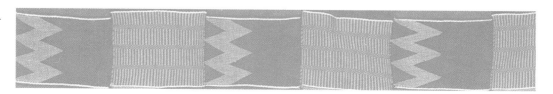

LAMB KEBABS

Brochettes d'Agneau

SERVES 4

Marinade

2 Tbsp • 25 mL	olive oil
2 Tbsp • 25 mL	lemon juice
1 Tbsp • 15 mL	minced flat-leaf parsley
1 Tbsp • 15 mL	paprika
1 tsp • 5 mL	ground cumin
1 tsp • 5 mL	ground coriander
1 tsp • 5 mL	garlic paste
1 tsp • 5 mL	salt
1 tsp • 5 mL	freshly ground black pepper

Kebabs

2 lb • 1 kg	boneless leg of lamb, cut into 1-inch (2.5-cm) cubes
8	long metal skewers
	olive oil for basting

1 Combine all marinade ingredients in a large bowl. Add lamb and toss well to coat thoroughly. Cover and marinate in the refrigerator overnight.

2 Remove lamb and thread 6–8 pieces onto each skewer.

3 Grill skewers over medium-high heat for about 4 minutes per side, turning and basting with olive oil frequently.

4 Serve with couscous or French bread and *harissa* (recipe page 224).

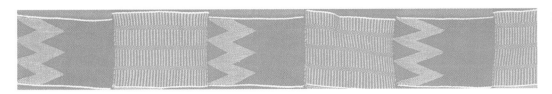

Spicy BEEF KEBABS
Kyinkyinga

Marinade

2	large onions, grated
2 Tbsp • 25 mL	white vinegar
1 Tbsp • 15 mL	tomato paste
1 Tbsp • 15 mL	chili paste or *sambal oelek* (see page 231)
2 tsp • 10 mL	ginger paste
1 tsp • 5 mL	garlic paste
2 Tbsp • 25 mL	ground dry-roasted peanuts

Kebabs

2 lb • 1 kg	beef steak (fillet, sirloin, rump), cut into 1-inch (2.5-cm) cubes
2	large green or red bell peppers, cut into 1-inch (2.5-cm) squares
2 Tbsp • 25 mL	ground dry-roasted peanuts
12	long metal skewers

1 Mix all marinade ingredients in a non-reactive bowl. Add beef cubes and toss well to coat. Cover and marinate overnight in the refrigerator.

2 Remove meat from the marinade and thread 5–6 beef cubes alternating with peppers onto each skewer.

3 Grill on high heat for about 4 minutes per side. Sprinkle ground peanut powder over cooked kebabs.

4 Serve with salad or rice.

• *Pronounced* chin-chin-ga, *traditional kebabs include beef and liver and are a common street food in Mali, Cameroon and a few other West African countries.*

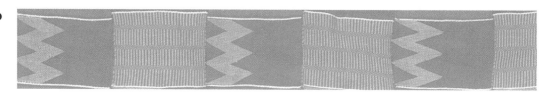

Ground LAMB KEBABS

Brochette de Kufta

SERVES 5–10

2	medium onions, coarsely chopped
½ cup • 125 mL	chopped flat-leaf parsley
½ cup • 125 mL	chopped cilantro leaves
2 Tbsp • 25 mL	chopped mint leaves
1 Tbsp • 15 mL	chopped marjoram leaves
1 Tbsp • 15 mL	paprika
2 tsp • 10 mL	chopped garlic
2 tsp • 10 mL	ground cumin
1 tsp • 5 mL	crushed chili flakes
½ tsp • 2.5 mL	ground allspice
½ tsp • 2.5 mL	*ras el-hanout* (see page 230)
1 tsp • 5 mL	salt
2 lb • 1 kg	ground lamb or beef (double-ground)
10	long, flat, metal skewers
	vegetable oil or melted butter for basting

1 Blend onion, herbs, spices and salt in a blender or food processor. Add ground meat to blended mixture and mix thoroughly with hands. Cover and refrigerate for at least 4 hours, or preferably overnight, to develop flavors.

2 Divide meat mixture into 20 small balls. Using 2 meatballs per skewer, form sausages around skewers at least 4 inches (10 cm) long. Pinch the sausage all along its length to ensure meat adheres to skewers.

3 Grill over high heat, turning and basting frequently with oil or melted butter, for about 5–6 minutes or until cooked.

4 Serve with *ksra* bread (see page 229) or pita bread and tomato-onion salad.

• *Although ground mutton or beef* kefta *are popular street fare throughout Morocco, if one is sampling these kebabs in the souks—a labyrinth of covered alleyways—they will probably be made of less expensive camel meat and fat.*

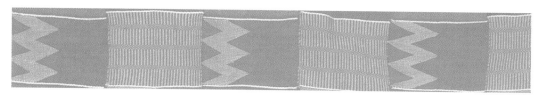

MARRAKECH LAMB kebabs

Al kotban Mrakchiya

Marinade

¼ cup • 50 mL	olive oil
¼ cup • 50 mL	lemon juice
1 Tbsp • 15 mL	paprika
1 Tbsp • 15 mL	chopped garlic
2 Tbsp • 25 mL	chopped cilantro leaves
2 Tbsp • 25 mL	chopped flat-leaf parsley
1 tsp • 5 mL	ground cumin
1 tsp • 5 mL	ground coriander
1 tsp • 5 mL	freshly ground black pepper
1 tsp • 5 mL	*harissa* (recipe page 224) or crushed red chilies

Kebabs

2 lb • 1 kg	boneless leg of lamb, trimmed of fat and cut into 1½-inch (4-cm) cubes
6	long metal skewers

1 Mix all marinade ingredients in a non-reactive bowl. Add lamb and stir well to ensure mixture coats each piece. Cover and marinate overnight in the refrigerator.

2 Remove lamb from marinade and reserve marinade. Thread about 8 lamb pieces onto each skewer and let it sit at room temperature for at least 30 minutes.

3 Grill over medium-high heat for about 4 minutes per side, turning occasionally and basting with marinade. The lamb should be brown on the outside and pink inside.

4 Serve on a bed of lettuce with mint leaves and lemon wedges. A side dish of tomato salsa and *ksra* bread (see page 229) often accompanies these kebabs.

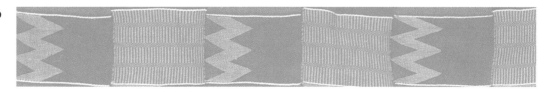

BEEF KEBABS

Koutbane or Qudban

SERVES 4–8 *Marinade*

2	medium onions, coarsely chopped
½ cup • 125 mL	chopped flat-leaf parsley
½ cup • 125 mL	chopped cilantro leaves
¼ cup • 50 mL	olive oil
¼ cup • 50 mL	lemon juice
1 Tbsp • 15 mL	paprika
1 tsp • 5 mL	garlic paste
1 tsp • 5 mL	ground cumin
1 tsp • 5 mL	ground coriander
1 tsp • 5 mL	freshly ground black pepper
½ tsp • 2.5 mL	chili powder
1 tsp • 5 mL	salt

Kebabs

2 lb • 1 kg	fillet of beef cut into 1-inch (2.5-cm) cube
1 lb • 500 g	beef suet cut into ½-inch (1-cm) pieces
8	long metal skewers

1 Blend marinade ingredients in a blender or a food processor and place in a non-reactive bowl. Add beef cubes and toss well to coat. Cover and marinate overnight in the refrigerator.

2 Remove beef and reserve marinade. Thread 6–8 beef cubes alternating with pieces of suet onto each skewer.

3 Grill on high heat, turning and basting frequently with reserved marinade, approximately 5–6 minutes for medium doneness.

4 Serve with warm *ksra* bread (see page 229), tomato-onion salad, and a mixture of salt, cumin and chili powders.

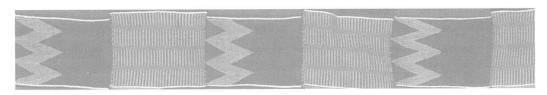

SWORDFISH KEBABS

Qudban del Hut

Marinade

1 cup • 250 mL	**flat-leaf parsley, finely minced**
4	**garlic cloves, finely minced**
2 Tbsp • 25 mL	**lemon juice**
2 Tbsp • 25 mL	**olive oil**
2 tsp • 10 mL	**ground cumin**
1 tsp • 5 mL	**crushed red chili flakes**
1 tsp • 5 mL	**salt**
	vegetable oil or melted butter for basting

Kebabs

2 lb • 1 kg	**swordfish fillets cut into 1-inch (2.5-cm) cubes**
16	**medium metal or presoaked wooden skewers**

1 Mix all marinade ingredients in a non-reactive bowl. Add fish and toss well to coat. Cover and marinate for 2 hours in the refrigerator, tossing every 30 minutes.

2 Thread about 4–5 fish cubes onto each skewer. Grill over medium heat, about 3–4 minutes per side, basting with vegetable oil or melted butter occasionally.

3 Serve over lettuce with *taratoor* (see page 231) and *charmoula* (recipe page 221).

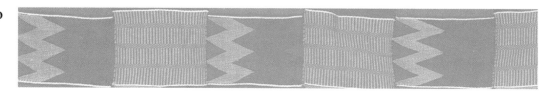

VEGETABLE KEBABS
Hodra Mechwya

SERVE 4

½	**medium head cauliflower separated into 1 inch (2.5 cm) florets**
2	**zucchini cut into 1-inch (2.5-cm) pieces**
1	**medium eggplant, peeled and cut into 1-inch (2.5-cm) pieces**
1	**red pepper, seeded and cut into 1-inch (2.5-cm) pieces**
1	**medium red onion, cut into 1-inch (2.5-cm) wedges and layers separated**
½ cup • 125 mL	*charmoula* **(recipe page 221)**
4	**thin, long, metal skewers**

1 Blanch cauliflower in boiling water for 1 minute; drain and pat dry.

2 In a large non-reactive bowl, combine all vegetables and the *charmoula*. Toss well, cover and marinate for 2−4 hours in the refrigerator.

3 Drain marinade and reserve. Thread vegetables onto skewers in an alternating fashion.

4 Grill over medium heat for about 6−8 minutes turning and basting with reserved marinade frequently.

5 When cooked, remove vegetables from skewers, sprinkle with salt and ground cumin and serve.

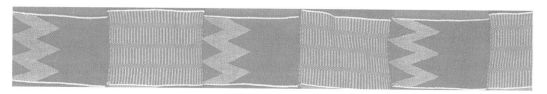

Spicy BEEF and LIVER KEBABS

Suya or Tsire

Marinade

2 Tbsp • 25 mL	lemon juice
1	medium onion, grated
¼ cup • 50 mL	vegetable oil
2 tsp • 10 mL	ginger paste
1 tsp • 5 mL	garlic paste
2 tsp • 10 mL	cayenne pepper
1 tsp • 5 mL	salt

Kebabs

1 lb • 500 g	beefsteak (top sirloin, round) cut into 1-inch (2.5-cm) cubes
1 lb • 500 g	beef liver cut into 1-inch (2.5-cm) cubes
1 cup • 250 mL	ground roasted peanuts
12	long metal skewers

1 Mix all marinade ingredients in a non-reactive bowl. Add beef and liver cubes, tossing well to ensure each piece is well coated. Cover and marinate in the refrigerator overnight.

2 Remove beef and liver from the marinade and reserve marinade. Thread the meat alternately onto the skewers and brush liberally with marinade.

3 Roll each skewer in ground peanuts to fully coat meat pieces. Grill over high heat for about 3 minutes per side.

4 Serve over rice or salad.

• *In northern Nigeria there is a variation of suya, called* killahi *or* balangu, *which uses mutton from goat or sheep marinated in a dry mixture of spices and peanut powder.*

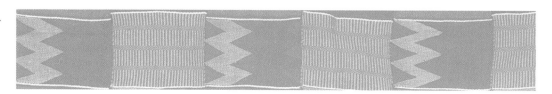

Spicy ground BEEF KEBABS

Tsiren Dakakken Nama

SERVES 6

1 lb • 500 g	lean ground beef
1	medium onion, finely chopped
1	egg, beaten
2 Tbsp • 25 mL	chopped cilantro
1 Tbsp • 15 mL	chili powder
1 tsp • 5 mL	nutmeg
½ tsp • 2.5 mL	salt
12	medium, thick, 4-sided metal skewers
	vegetable oil for basting

1 In a non-reactive bowl, mix ground beef with onion, egg, cilantro, chili powder, nutmeg and salt. Knead mixture well with hands, cover and let rest in the refrigerator overnight.

2 Divide the mixture into 12 equal balls. Moisten hands with water and wrap each ball around a metal skewer to form a 3–4 inch (7.5–10-cm) long sausage.

3 Grill over medium-high heat for 7–10 minutes, turning and basting frequently with oil.

4 Serve with onion salad and lemon wedges.

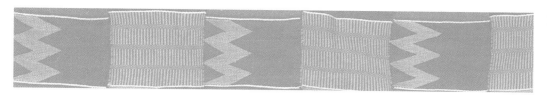

Spicy MUTTON KEBABS
Kiliahi or Balangu

Marinade

1 Tbsp • 15 mL	paprika
2 Tbsp • 25 mL	ground peanuts
1 Tbsp • 15 mL	cayenne pepper
1 Tbsp • 15 mL	dried onion flakes
1 tsp • 5 mL	powdered garlic
1 tsp • 5 mL	ginger powder
1 tsp • 5 mL	salt

Kebabs

1 lb • 500 g	mutton (sheep, lamb or goat) cut in thin slices
8	medium metal skewers
	vegetable oil for basting

1 Mix marinade ingredients and sprinkle over meat slices, coating each slice thoroughly. Let meat marinate for at least 30 minutes.

2 Thread mutton slices onto metal skewers. Grill over medium heat for about 4–5 minutes per side, basting with oil occasionally.

3 Serve with slices of onion and tomato.

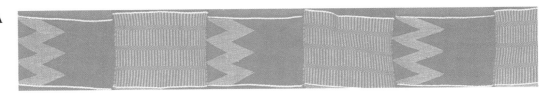

LAMB SKEWERS with apricots

Sosaties

Marinade

3 Tbsp • 45 mL	**vegetable oil**
1 cup • 250 mL	**finely chopped onion**
1 tsp • 5 mL	**garlic paste**
1 tsp • 5 mL	**ground cumin**
1 tsp • 5 mL	**ground coriander**
1 tsp • 5 mL	**chili powder**
2 Tbsp • 25 mL	**sugar**
1 cup • 250 mL	**white vinegar**
2 Tbsp • 25 mL	**apricot jam**
2 Tbsp • 25 mL	**soy sauce**
2 Tbsp • 25 mL	**red wine**
1 Tbsp • 15 mL	**tamarind paste**

Kebabs

2 lb • 1 kg	**boneless leg of lamb cut into 1-inch (2.5-cm) cubes**
½ lb • 225 g	**dried apricots, cut into halves**
½ cup • 125 mL	**dry sherry**
12	**long metal skewers**
2	**medium onions, cut into 1-inch (2.5-cm) pieces**

1 Heat oil in a pan over high heat and sauté onion until translucent, 4–5 minutes. Add garlic, cumin, coriander and chili powder. Sauté for 1 minute. Add sugar, vinegar, jam, soy sauce, wine and tamarind paste, and cook for 2 minutes on medium heat. Cool the mixture.

2 Place marinade in a non-reactive bowl. Add lamb cubes and toss well. Marinate in the refrigerator for 24–48 hours.

3 A day before grilling, soak dried apricot halves in sherry, cover and store in the refrigerator until needed.

4 Drain lamb and reserve marinade. Thread lamb onto skewers, alternating with onion pieces and apricot halves.

5 Grill over high heat for about 4 minutes per side, basting frequently with a mixture of half oil and half water.

6 Boil reserved marinade for about 5 minutes and serve as sauce.

• *Sosaties made of lamb, pork, chicken or seafood are popular fare in South African outdoor cookouts, known as* braai, *an abbreviation of* braaivleis—*an Afrikaner term meaning grilled meat.*

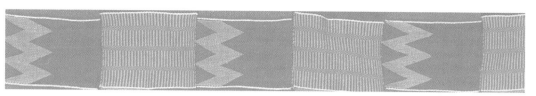

CHICKEN KEBABS

Chicken Sosaties

Marinade

¼ cup • 50 mL	fried onion
¼ cup • 50 mL	lemon juice
1 Tbsp • 15 mL	vegetable oil
1 Tbsp • 15 mL	brown sugar
1 Tbsp • 15 mL	soy sauce
1 tsp • 5 mL	garlic paste
1 tsp • 5 mL	ground coriander

Kebabs

1 lb • 500 g	boneless chicken breast or thigh cut into 1-inch (2.5-cm) cubes
8	medium metal or presoaked wooden skewers

1 Process marinade ingredients in a blender. Pour over chicken pieces and toss well to coat each piece. Transfer to a sealable plastic bag and marinate in the refrigerator for at least 4 hours or preferably overnight.

2 Drain marinade and reserve. Thread about 5–6 chicken pieces onto each skewer. Grill over medium heat for 3–4 minutes per side, turning and basting frequently with marinade.

3 Serve as appetizers with apricot chutney on the side.

• *Traditional sosaties use lamb and pork and require 2–3 days of marinating, but now chicken, fish and prawn sosaties are popular at South African* braaivleis *(barbecue parties).*

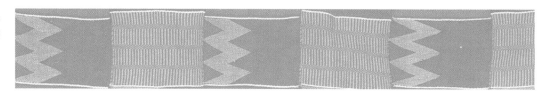

SWAHILI SHISH KEBABS

Mishkaki

SERVES 6

Marinade

2 Tbsp • 25 mL	vegetable oil
1 Tbsp • 15 mL	tomato paste
1 Tbsp • 15 mL	tamarind paste
1 tsp • 5 mL	curry powder
1 tsp • 5 mL	garlic paste
1 tsp • 5 mL	ginger paste
½ tsp • 2.5 mL	freshly ground black pepper
1 tsp • 5 mL	salt
	garam masala (recipe page 227) for sprinkling

Kebabs

2 lb • 1 kg	boneless beef or chicken breasts, cut into 1-inch (2.5-cm) cubes
12	medium metal skewers

1 In a non-reactive bowl, mix all marinade ingredients. Add meat pieces, and toss well to coat. Cover and marinate overnight in the refrigerator.

2 Remove meat from marinade and thread 5–6 pieces onto each skewer.

3 Grill over high heat for 3–4 minutes per side. When cooked, sprinkle with *garam masala*.

4. Serve with onion and tomato salad.

• *A variety of meat, fish and seafood kebabs are sold in open-air food stalls in Jamituri Gardens close to Stonetown in Zanzibar. Hordes of locals and visitors gather at sundown to savor these treats.*

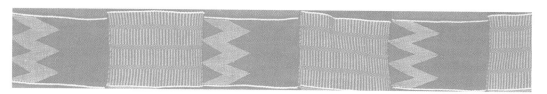

LAMB KEBABS

Brochettes d'agneau

Marinade

1 Tbsp • 15 mL	**paprika**
2 Tbsp • 25 mL	**lemon juice**
2 Tbsp • 25 mL	**olive oil**
1 Tbsp • 15 mL	**minced flat-leaf parsley**
1 tsp • 5 mL	**ground cumin**
1 tsp • 5 mL	**ground coriander**
1 tsp • 5 mL	**garlic paste**
1 tsp • 5 mL	**crushed red pepper flakes**
1 tsp • 5 mL	**salt**
1 tsp • 5 mL	**freshly ground black pepper**

Kebabs

2 lb • 1 kg	**boneless leg of lamb, cut into 1-inch (2.5-cm) cubes**
12	**long metal skewers**
6	**medium tomatoes, each cut into 8 wedges**

1 Mix marinade ingredients in a non-reactive bowl. Add lamb pieces and toss to ensure every piece is coated with marinade. Marinate in the refrigerator for at least 4 hours or preferably overnight.

2 Remove lamb from marinade, reserving marinade. Thread 5–6 pieces on each skewer alternating with tomato wedges.

3 Grill kebabs over medium-high heat about 4 minutes per side, occasionally brushing with marinade. Remove skewers from heat and let rest for 5 minutes.

4 Serve with salad or rice pilaf and *harissa* (recipe page 224).

• *These kebabs are also sold at street stalls in Algeria and Morocco.*

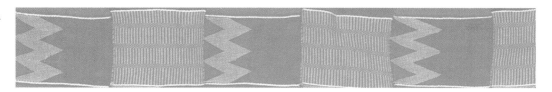

Spicy BEEF KEBABS

Mechoui

SERVES 6

Marinade

3 Tbsp • 45 mL	olive oil
4 Tbsp • 50 mL	lemon juice
1 Tbsp • 15 mL	*harissa* (recipe page 224)
1	medium onion, grated or finely minced
2 tsp • 10 mL	minced garlic
2 tsp • 10 mL	ground cumin
1½ tsp • 7.5 mL	paprika
1 tsp • 5 mL	red pepper flakes
½ tsp • 2.5 mL	ground cinnamon
½ tsp • 2.5 mL	freshly ground black pepper

Kebabs

2 lb • 1 kg	boneless beef (top sirloin, top round) cut into 1½-inch (4-cm) cubes
4	2 red and 2 green bell peppers, seeded and cut into 1½-inch (4-cm) pieces
2	medium onions, cut into 1½-inch (4-cm) wedges

12	long metal skewers
	salt
	olive oil for basting
2 Tbsp • 25 mL	chopped cilantro for garnish

1 Mix marinade ingredients in a non-reactive bowl. Add meat pieces and toss well to coat thoroughly. Marinate in the refrigerator for at least 4 hours and preferably overnight.

2 Remove meat pieces from marinade, reserving marinade. Thread 6–8 pieces of beef on each of 6 skewers and thread vegetable pieces separately on the remaining 6 skewers. Sprinkle with salt.

3 Grill beef on high heat for about 3–4 minutes per side, basting with marinade only once while turning. Brush vegetable skewers with olive oil and grill on high heat for 2 minutes per side or until slightly charred.

4 Sprinkle with chopped cilantro. Serve over saffron rice or in pita bread.

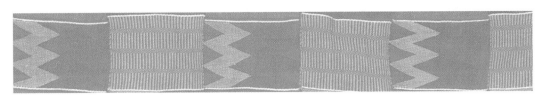

BEEF KEBABS

Tsitsinga

½ cup • 125 mL	vegetable oil
2 Tbsp • 25 mL	red wine vinegar
1 tsp • 5 mL	salt
1 lb • 500 g	lean beefsteak, cut into 1-inch (2.5-cm) cubes
1	medium onion, coarsely chopped
2-inch • 5-cm	piece fresh ginger
4	fresh green chilies, seeded
1	medium tomato
8	medium metal or presoaked wooden skewers
½ cup • 125 mL	roasted cornmeal

1 Mix vegetable oil, red wine vinegar and salt. Add beef cubes and toss well to coat. Marinate for at least 2 hours.

2 Purée onion, ginger, chilies and tomato in a blender and set aside.

3 Remove meat from marinade and thread 4–5 pieces onto each skewer. Grill over high heat until half cooked, about 2 minutes per side.

4 Roll each skewer in vegetable purée so beef pieces are fully coated. Roll coated skewers in cornmeal. Grill again for another 2 minutes per side or until cooked.

5 Serve with rice, salad and a hot sauce.

• *To roast cornmeal place in a dry frying pan over medium heat, stirring constantly until a golden brown color is obtained. Be careful not to let it burn.*

Central and South Asia

This region includes Iran, Afghanistan, the Central Asian Republics of the former Soviet Union, and the entire Indian subcontinent, including Pakistan, Bangladesh, Burma (Myanmar) and Sri Lanka. Although geographically and politically recognized as a part of the Middle East, Iran has much stronger culinary affinities with the countries of Central and South Asia than with the Middle East, hence its inclusion in this chapter. The countries here not only share similar cooking characteristics and styles, they also have a common culinary vocabulary that is predominantly Persian in origin.

Not long ago the Central Asian Republics of Kazakhstan, Uzbekistan, Turkmenistan, Tajikistan and Kyrgyzstan were part of the Soviet Union and not well known to the outside world. After the dissolution of the Soviet Union in 1991, however, they became independent countries. The population of these countries is predominantly Muslim and the food and its preparation are generally similar, partly based on the nomadic life and partly Turkish and Persian. Meat is the foundation of most dishes and although mutton is preferred, goat, beef, chicken, horse and camel are also consumed. Shashlyk or kebabs served with *plov* (rice pilaf)

or round, oven-baked, flatbread called *non* or *lipioshka* (see page 229) are very much part of the daily diet, and the aroma of grilled kebabs and freshly baked bread fills the air in marketplaces throughout these countries. In the tea shops, or *chaikhanas*, that are traditional gathering places mainly for men, particularly in Uzbekistan, Turkmenistan and Afghanistan, very inexpensive kebabs can be had with rice or local traditional bread and washed down with endless cups of black or green tea.

Central Asian kebabs are not very spicy and seasonings are simple, consisting mainly of cumin, coriander, red or black pepper, barberries, wine vinegar, parsley, cilantro, dill and basil. Fat is often inserted between pieces of skewered meat to add flavor and keep it from drying out during grilling. Unlike Europe, the Middle East and North Africa, where it is a common practice to use leftover marinade to baste the kebabs while grilling, in Central and South Asia specially prepared basting liquids, oil or melted butter are often used.

The word kebab, and its several variants, is derived from the Persian word *kabab*, which generally means food that is threaded onto a skewer and grilled over an open fire. There are, however, a variety of preparations in Iran and in the Indian subcontinent that do not require skewers or grilling over an open fire and yet are referred to as kebabs; they may be deep-fried, shallow-fried, broiled, steamed or boiled. Kebab cookery has long been one of the hallmarks of Persian cuisine, as is evident by its popularity among Iranians and the presence of hundreds of street vendors, *kabab-khaneh* (kebab houses) and restaurants offering kebabs in Iran. Persian kebabs have a subtle flavor achieved by using simple marinades consisting only of lemon juice, olive oil, onion, garlic, saffron and sometimes yogurt. Marinating time for Persian kebabs tends to be much longer— 2 to 3 days in the refrigerator is not unusual.

Lamb, beef, chicken and fish kebabs are popular but *chelou kabab* tops them all and is considered the national dish of Iran. Chelou refers to buttered rice baked in an oven until it forms a golden crusty bottom called *tahdig*. The kebabs can be of any meat except pork but preferably the loin or leg of lamb. Although several regional variations exist, Tehran-style *chelou kababs* are prepared from boneless pieces of leg or shoulder of lamb that are marinated in a mixture of onion juice, yogurt, lemon juice and freshly ground black pepper for at least 12 hours and up to two days. The grilled skewers are served over steaming *chelou* with raw egg yolk and melted butter and a liberal sprinkling of sumac powder. The dish is often accompanied by grilled tomato and

herbs such as mint. A wide variety of kebabs enrich the Iranian culinary repertoire but the most popular ones are *koobideh* (ground lamb), *joojeh* (chicken), *barg* (fillet of beef or lamb), *chenjeh* (lamb), *maahi* (fish) and *kolbeh* (mixed grill).

The cuisine of Afghanistan is very much influenced by the cooking of Iran, Pakistan, India and, to some extent, Mongolia. Despite the fact that Afghanistan once shared its border with Russian-controlled Central Asian republics, there appears to be no evidence of Russian culinary influence in Afghani cuisine. Indian spices, mint and yogurt are important ingredients in Afghani cuisine but spices and seasoning are used sparingly in order not to overwhelm the natural flavor of the meat. As in Central Asian republics, the social life of men in Afghanistan revolves around teahouses *(chaikhana)*, where local women are seldom seen. There are very few western-style restaurants, and Afghans prefer to frequent teahouses and the numerous street stalls that sell inexpensive kebabs and snacks.

Historically there has been a high degree of cultural interaction between Persia and India. Persian influence in the Indian subcontinent goes as far back as the 10th century when Persian invaders occupied northwest India. Thereafter a wave of other Muslim invaders, mostly Turkish and Afghani in origin, extended Muslim rule to other parts of the subcontinent. The latter, although not ethnically Persian, became propagators of Indo-Persian interaction particularly in the areas of language and literature. During the Moghul Empire that prevailed from 1526 to 1707 in most of India, Islam as a religion was consolidated in South Asia, and Persian-inspired architecture, art, literature, music and culinary practices flourished, particularly in north and central India. The Moghuls adopted Persian as their court language and established Moghul cooking—a fusion between Persian and Indian styles that is firmly established even today as Moghul or Mughalai cuisine.

Although historical evidence points to a type of kebab cookery in the Indian subcontinent as far back as 400 BC, food historians in India claim that much before the advent of Muslim influence, the Rajput warriors of Rajasthan consumed kebabs known as *mass ke suley*, made from game cooked or smoked over an open wood fire. However, the credit for introducing the Persian-, Arabic- and Turkish-inspired art of kebab cookery in South Asia must surely go to the Moghuls who introduced the clay tandoor oven from Central Asia, now the mainstay of Indian-style tandoori grilling. Meat, poultry, seafood, bread or anything else cooked in a tandoor transforms food into a unique and unforgettable culinary experience. A typical tandoor oven used in India is a beehive-shaped, hollow clay pot standing about 5 feet (1.5 m) high and heated by wood or charcoal. Heat from smoldering embers and radiating from the clay walls provides a temperature gradient that can be used to cook a variety of foods. Spicy marinated meats are threaded onto long iron skewers and cooked just above the embers at the bottom. The extremely high temperatures exceeding 500°F (260°C), not only sears the meat to trap the spices and natural juices but also cooks the meat very fast. The food is cooked on the outside and remains moist on the inside with the distinctive flavor and smoky aroma so characteristic of tandoori grilling.

The Indian subcontinent is where kebab cookery has attained its highest degree of sophistication and innovation. There are probably two reasons for this: the availability of a vast array of exotic spices and herbs; and the use of goat, sheep, pig, beef, wild boar, deer, chicken, ducks, game birds, marine and freshwater fish and crustaceans as well as traditional lamb. Despite limitations imposed by religious beliefs to exclude one or the other type of meat, kebab culture in South Asia is firmly established and, in fact, is expanding as fast-food outlets have become fashionable among a sizable emerging affluent middle- and upper-class population.

Spices are at the heart of Indian cooking, and their specific uses in different parts of the country along with climatic, geographical and religious characteristics form the basis of regional diversity in this vast country. There is, however, a north-south culinary divide within the country. The cooking style of the north reflects Middle Eastern and Central Asian influences, with meat and bread as staples, whereas southern cuisine is characterized by rice, vegetables, fish and spicy curries. The cuisines of North India and Pakistan are so similar that it is difficult to assign a country of origin to some dishes. Pakistan is primarily a Muslim country and pork is avoided, but beef is incorporated into some dishes, unlike in India.

Kebab cookery in most parts of the world has generally been associated with Muslim populations and India is no exception. In India it has long been a domain of Muslim cooks who established centers of culinary excellence under the patronage of royal princes and nawabs creating a rich repertoire of kebabs and other meat preparations. Two such centers are worth mentioning. One in the north of India, in the city of Lucknow, is devoted to the Avadhi style of cooking, which involves low fire, slow cooking and use of rare spices to produce subtle flavors. The other in Hyderabad, in south India, specializes in Hyderabadi culinary style which incorporates nuts and select spices and herbs to give rich and aromatic character to the food. Avadhi master chefs have created culinary delicacies such as *galouti* or *galavat kabab* and *kakori kabab*, whereas Hyderabadi cuisine has contributed an assortment of kebab preparations such as *husseini kabab, kacche kabab, patthar kabab* and *shikampuri kabab* to the Indian culinary scene. Other popular preparations such as *shami kababs, chapli kabab* and *bihari kabab* are irresistible options for kebab connoisseurs in the India subcontinent.

Other South Asian countries, such as Bangladesh, Burma (Myanmar), Sri Lanka, Nepal and Bhutan are not known for their indigenous kebabs. Bangladesh, which was carved out of the predominantly Muslim part of the Indian province of Bengal, shares culinary roots with the rest of Bengal. Although kebabs are widely available in stalls and restaurants, they are not distinctive and tend to be poor copies of their Indian counterpart. Burmese cuisine blends the ingredients and cooking styles of India and China and, to a lesser extent, Thailand. In two major cities, Rangoon and Mandalay, Chinese and Indian restaurants outnumber indigenous Burmese restaurants. Kebabs are not a major component of Burmese cuisine and tend to be Indian in style as kebabs were introduced by Indian Muslims who had settled in Burma (Myanmar) long ago. One popular street food in Rangoon is pork threaded on a bamboo skewer, called *wat thar dote htoe*, which is dipped in a sweet spicy boiling sauce before eating. In Sri Lanka, kebabs are not generally seen as a street food; however, they are available in some restaurants catering to tourists or in food stalls in mostly Muslim-populated areas.

CHICKEN KEBABS

Mourgh kabaub

SERVES 6

Marinade

½ cup • 125 mL	yogurt
1 tsp • 5 mL	garlic paste
1 tsp • 5 mL	ground coriander
1 tsp • 5 mL	ground cumin
1 tsp • 5 mL	salt
½ tsp • 2.5 mL	freshly ground black pepper
½ tsp • 2.5 mL	turmeric

Kebabs

2 lb • 1 kg	boneless chicken breast or thigh, cut into 1½-inch (4-cm) pieces
1	medium red onion, quartered and layers separated
2	green bell peppers, seeded and cut into 1½-inches (4-cm) squares
12	long metal skewers
¼ cup • 50 mL	vegetable oil for basting
12	cherry tomatoes

1 Combine all marinade ingredients in a non-reactive bowl. Add chicken pieces and toss well to coat. Cover and marinate in the refrigerator overnight.

2 Thread 4–5 pieces of chicken alternating with onion and green pepper onto each skewer.

3. Grill over medium-high heat for about 3–4 minutes per side, turning and basting with oil frequently.

4. Thread one cherry tomato at the top of each skewer before serving over rice pilaf *(palow)* or with Afghani flat bread *(naan, see page 229)*.

SKEWERED CHICKEN

Kyethar Ghin

Marinade

SERVES 6

2 Tbsp • 25 mL	vegetable oil
1 Tbsp • 15 mL	finely minced lemon grass (white portion)
1 Tbsp • 15 mL	lemon juice
1 tsp • 5 mL	garlic paste
1 tsp • 5 mL	paprika
1 tsp • 5 mL	salt
1 tsp • 5 mL	soy sauce
1 tsp • 5 mL	fish sauce
½ tsp • 2.5 mL	turmeric powder

Kebabs

2 lb • 1 kg	boneless, skinless chicken breast cut into 1-inch (2.5-cm) cubes
12	medium presoaked bamboo skewers
¼ cup • 50 mL	vegetable oil for basting

1 Combine all marinade ingredients in a non-reactive bowl. Add chicken cubes and toss well to coat. Cover and marinate in the refrigerator for at least 4 hours or preferably overnight.

2 Remove chicken from marinade. Thread 5–6 pieces onto each skewer, leaving a small space between them.

3 Grill over medium heat for 3 minutes. Baste with vegetable oil before grilling the other side for 3 more minutes.

4 Serve with a simple tomato, onion and lettuce salad or with Burmese salad *(ah thoke)* with Burmese seasoning, or a simple tomato, onion and lettuce salad.

• *Burmese salads* (ah thoke) *consists of fresh cabbage, carrots, lettuce, cilantro, onion and tomato and is usually seasoned with a complex Burmese dressing made of lime juice, tamarind juice, fish sauce, chili oil, pounded dried prawns, crushed peanuts, sesame seeds and gram flour.*

Spicy BEEF KEBABS

Ahmaithar Ghin

Marinade

½ cup • 125 mL	yogurt
¼ cup • 50 mL	vegetable oil
¼ cup • 50 mL	lemon juice
2 Tbsp • 25 mL	ground cumin
1 Tbsp • 15 mL	ground coriander
1 tsp • 5 mL	ground cardamom
1 tsp • 5 mL	chili powder
1 tsp • 5 mL	paprika
1 tsp • 5 mL	turmeric
1 tsp • 5 mL	salt

Kebabs

2 lb • 1 kg	boneless lean beef, cut into 1½-inch (4-cm) pieces
8	medium presoaked bamboo skewers

1 Combine all marinade ingredients in a bowl. Add beef and toss well to coat each piece. Cover and marinate in the refrigerator for up to 24 hours.

2 Drain marinade and reserve. Thread beef pieces onto full length of each skewer, leaving little or no wood exposed to the fire.

3 Grill over high heat, frequently turning and basting with reserved marinade for 8–10 minutes.

4 Serve with rice or salad.

• *Ghin in Burmese refers to skewer, and* ahmai *is the meat from water buffalo, which is traditionally used in these kebabs.*

FISH KEBABS

Machchi Kabab

Marinade

1 cup • 250 mL	yogurt
¼ cup • 50 mL	finely chopped cilantro
2 Tbsp • 25 mL	besan (gram flour)
2 Tbsp • 25 mL	lemon juice
2 tsp • 10 mL	ground coriander
1 tsp • 5 mL	ground cumin
1 tsp • 5 mL	garam masala
1 tsp • 5 mL	ajwain (carom seeds)
1 tsp • 5 mL	garlic paste
1 tsp • 5 mL	ginger paste
1½ tsp • 7.5 mL	salt
½ tsp • 2.5 mL	turmeric
½ tsp • 2.5 mL	chili powder

Kebabs

2 lb • 1 kg	firm white fish fillets, cut into 1½-inch (4-cm) pieces
8	medium thin metal or pre soaked bamboo skewers
¼ cup • 50 mL	melted butter or ghee for basting

SERVES 8 AS AN APPETIZER, 4 AS MAIN COURSE

1 Mix all marinade ingredients in a non-reactive bowl. Add fish pieces and toss gently to coat. Marinate for up to 2 hours in the refrigerator.

2 Thread 5–6 pieces of fish onto each skewer, leaving ½-inch (1-cm) space between them.

3 Grill over medium heat for about 3–4 minutes per side, basting frequently with melted butter or ghee.

4 Serve with sliced onion, lemon and tomato wedges.

• *Besan, also known as gram flour, chana flour or chickpea flour has a slightly nutty flavor and is an important ingredient in Indian cooking. Ajwain seeds, also known as carom seeds look like cumin or fennel seeds but have a strikingly stronger caraway- or thyme-like flavor. They are used in many Indian and African dishes.*

• *Ghee, is Indian clarified butter without any milk solids or water. It is used extensively throughout south Asia to enrich flavors of sweet and savory foods.*

• *Garam masala is a spice blend (recipe page 227).*

• *All the above items are available in stores where Indian food and spices are sold.*

LAMB KEBABS

Boti Kabab

SERVES 4

Marinade

½ cup • 125 mL	yogurt
¼ cup • 50 mL	lemon juice
1 Tbsp • 15 mL	tomato paste
2 tsp • 10 mL	ground coriander
2 tsp • 10 mL	ground cumin
2 tsp • 10 mL	ginger paste
2 tsp • 10 mL	garlic paste
1 tsp • 5 mL	salt
½ tsp • 2.5 mL	turmeric
½ tsp • 2.5 mL	green cardamom powder
½ tsp • 2.5 mL	ground cloves
½ tsp • 2.5 mL	ground cinnamon
½ tsp • 2.5 mL	ground nutmeg
½ tsp • 2.5 mL	cayenne pepper

Kebabs

2 lb • 1 kg	boneless leg of lamb cut into 1½-inch (4-cm) cubes
8	long metal skewers
¼ cup • 50 mL	melted butter or vegetable oil for basting
	garam masala for sprinkling

1 Combine all marinade ingredients in a non-reactive bowl. Add lamb cubes and toss well to coat thoroughly. Cover and marinate in the refrigerator for at least 4 hours but preferably overnight.

2 Thread 5–6 pieces of lamb onto each skewer leaving a gap of about ¼-inch (.5-cm) between pieces. Grill on high heat for 2 minutes per side. Brush with oil or butter, lower heat to medium and continue grilling and turning for another 8–10 minutes or until meat is browned on all sides. Brush again with melted butter or oil. Sprinkle with garam masala.

3 Serve with rice pilaf or onion, tomato and radish salad.

CREAMY CHICKEN KEBABS

Murgh Malai Kabab

Marinade

¼ cup • 50 mL	whipping cream
1 Tbsp • 15 mL	lemon juice
1 tsp • 5 mL	garlic paste
1 tsp • 5 mL	ginger paste
1 tsp • 5 mL	salt
1 tsp • 5 mL	ground white pepper
½ tsp • 2.5 mL	green cardamom powder
½ tsp • 2.5 mL	ground mace
½ tsp • 2.5 mL	ground nutmeg

Kebabs

16	chicken breast tenders
16	medium presoaked wooden skewers
¼ cup • 50 mL	melted butter for basting

1 Combine all marinade ingredients, mixing well and set aside.

2 Insert a wooden skewer along the length of each chicken tender. Place skewers in a glass or plastic tray with a lid.

3 Pour marinade over skewers. Cover and marinate for 5–6 hours in the refrigerator.

4 Bring kebabs to room temperature. Grill over medium heat for about 4 minutes, turning and basting with melted butter frequently.

5 Serve as appetizers straight off the grill, with mint or cilantro chutney.

• *These are perhaps the most delicate of the appetizer kebabs. I ate these in an unpretentious roadside restaurant on the outskirts of the city of Hyderabad in India.*

CHICKEN TIKKA KEBABS

Murgh Tikka

Marinade

½ cup • 125 mL	yogurt
2 Tbsp • 25 mL	vegetable oil
1 tsp • 5 mL	ground coriander
1 tsp • 5 mL	ground cumin
1 tsp • 5 mL	garlic paste
1 tsp • 5 mL	ginger paste
½ tsp • 2.5 mL	*garam masala* (recipe page 227)
½ tsp • 2.5 mL	cayenne pepper
¼ tsp • 1 mL	turmeric
¼ tsp • 1 mL	ground nutmeg
⅛ tsp • .5 mL	tandoori orange-red food color

Kebabs

2 Tbsp • 25 mL	lemon juice
1 tsp • 5 mL	salt
1 lb • 500 g	boneless chicken thighs, cut into 1½-inch (4-cm) pieces
2	thin, long, metal skewers
¼ cup • 50 mL	each of vegetable oil and water mixture for basting

1 Combine lemon juice and salt in a non-reactive bowl, add chicken pieces and toss well to combine. Marinate in the refrigerator for at least 1 hour.

2 In another non-reactive bowl, combine marinade ingredients thoroughly to obtain a smooth paste. Add chicken, along with any juices, to the paste. Mix well to coat each piece. Cover and marinate in the refrigerator overnight.

3 Thread about 8–10 chicken pieces onto each skewer. Grill over medium heat, turning frequently and basting with oil and water mixture occasionally for 6–8 minutes. Let cooked chicken skewers rest for 2–3 minutes.

4 Remove chicken from skewers and serve over a bed of raw sliced onions with lemon wedges.

• *This is my own recipe that has been a favorite with family and friends for a number of years. Here a tandoori marinade is used and the chicken undergoes a two-stage marinating process. Tandoori food color is available from stores selling Indian spices.*

Goanese PORK KEBABS
Espetada

As a former colony of Portugal, the Indian state of Goa incorporated many Portuguese dishes into its culinary repertoire. These kebabs are a Goanese version of Portuguese *espetada*.

Marinade

SERVES 4

¼ cup • 50 mL	white vinegar
2	dry red chilies
2	fresh green chilies
20	peppercorns
6	cloves
6–8	garlic cloves
1-inch • 2.5-cm	piece fresh ginger
1-inch • 2.5-cm	cinnamon stick
2 Tbsp • 25 mL	vegetable oil
2 Tbsp • 25 mL	chopped cilantro
1½ tsp • 7.5 mL	salt
1 tsp • 5 mL	cumin seeds
½ tsp • 2.5 mL	turmeric

Kebabs

2 lb • 1 kg	pork loin, cut into 1½-inch (4-cm) cubes
8	long metal skewers
¼ cup • 50 mL	vegetable oil or melted butter for basting

1 Grind all marinade ingredients in a food processor. Transfer the paste to a non-reactive bowl. Add pork cubes and toss well to coat. Cover and marinate in the refrigerator overnight.

2 Remove meat from the marinade. Thread 5–6 pieces onto each skewer.

3 Grill over medium heat for about 10 minutes, turning frequently and basting with oil or butter occasionally.

4 Serve with rice or salad.

CHICKEN KEBABS

Reshmi Kabab

SERVES 4–8

Marinade

10	**cashew nuts**
4	**green chilies, seeded**
2 Tbsp • 25 mL	**chopped mint**
2 Tbsp • 25 mL	**chopped cilantro**
1 tsp • 5 mL	**garlic paste**
1 tsp • 5 mL	**ginger paste**
1	**egg**
¼ cup • 50 mL	**whipping cream**

Kebabs

¼ cup • 50 mL	**lemon juice**
1 tsp • 5 mL	**salt**
2 lb • 1 kg	**boneless, skinless chicken breasts, cut into 1½-inch (4-cm) cubes**
8	**medium metal skewers**
¼ cup • 50 mL	**melted butter or ghee for basting**

1 Dissolve salt in lemon juice and pour over chicken cubes in a non-reactive bowl. Toss well and let marinate for at least 1 hour.

2 Grind cashew nuts, chilies, mint, cilantro, garlic, ginger and egg in a food processor. Transfer the paste to a non-reactive bowl. Add chicken pieces along with marinade juices and pour in cream. Mix well to coat each piece thoroughly. Cover and marinate in the refrigerator for at least 4 hours or preferably overnight.

3 Thread 5–6 chicken cubes onto each skewer and grill over medium heat for about 3 minutes per side, basting with melted butter while turning.

4 Serve with rice pilaf or *naan* (see page 229) and tomato and onion salad.

• *In Hindi,* reshmi *means "silken," and these kebabs are reputed to be as soft and smooth as silk.*

Ground CHICKEN KEBABS
Murgh Kheema Kabab

SERVES 4–8

1	**medium onion, coarsely chopped**
2	**green chilies, seeded**
¼ cup • 50 mL	**cashew nuts**
1	**egg**
1 Tbsp • 15 mL	**vegetable oil**
½ cup • 125 mL	**finely chopped cilantro**
1 Tbsp • 15 mL	**garlic paste**
1 Tbsp • 15 mL	**ginger paste**
1 tsp • 5 mL	**ground cumin**
1 tsp • 5 mL	**ground coriander**
1 tsp • 5 mL	**salt**
1 tsp • 5 mL	**garam masala**
½ tsp • 2.5 mL	**ground green cardamom**
½ tsp • 2.5 mL	**freshly ground black pepper**
2 lb • 1 kg	**ground chicken**
8	**long, metal skewers (4-sided or flat)**
	melted butter for basting

1 Purée onion, chilies, cashews, egg and oil in a blender. Place the paste in a non-reactive bowl and combine with seasonings and chicken. Knead to form a firm mixture. Cover and refrigerate overnight.

2 Divide the mixture into 8 portions. Moisten hands with water, wrap each portion around a skewer to form a long sausage about 1-inch (2.5-cm) in diameter.

3 Grill skewers over medium heat, turning frequently until uniformly golden brown on all sides, 6–8 minutes. Baste with melted butter.

4 Slide cooked kebabs off the skewers and serve with mint chutney, sliced raw onions and lemon wedges.

LAMB KEBABS

Chenjeh kabab

SERVES 4

2 lb • 1 kg	boneless leg of lamb, cut into 1½-inch (4-cm) cubes
2	medium onions, finely chopped or grated
½ cup • 125 mL	lime or lemon juice
1 tsp • 5 mL	salt
½ tsp • 2.5 mL	freshly ground black pepper
½ lb • 250 g	lamb fat, cut into 1-inch (2.5-cm) pieces
8	long, thin flat metal skewers
¼ cup • 50 mL	melted clarified butter or ghee
¼ cup • 50 mL	lime juice
½ tsp • 2.5 mL	ground saffron dissolved in 2 Tbsp (25 mL)water
½ tsp • 2.5 mL	salt
¼ tsp • 1.2 mL	freshly ground black pepper
	sumac for sprinkling

1 Combine lamb, onions, lime juice, salt and pepper in a non-reactive bowl. Toss well to coat. Cover and marinate at least overnight in the refrigerator.

2 Thread 5–6 pieces of lamb alternating with fat pieces onto each skewer.

3 Make a basting liquid by combining melted butter, lime juice, saffron, salt and black pepper.

4 Grill skewers on medium-heat for 3–4 minutes per side, basting while turning.

5 Remove cooked kebabs from skewers and serve them on *lavash* (see page 229) brushed with the basting liquid. Sprinkle with *sumac* (see page 231) and serve with grilled tomatoes.

FILLET or LEAF KEBABS

Kabab-e Barg

Marinade

1 cup • 250 mL	yogurt
½ cup • 125 mL	lime juice
juice of	**2 medium onions**
1 tsp • 5 mL	salt
1 tsp • 5 mL	freshly ground black pepper

Kebabs

2 lb • 1 kg	loin meat (beef, lamb or veal)
2 Tbsp • 25 mL	melted clarified butter
2 Tbsp • 25 mL	lime juice
½ tsp • 2.5 mL	salt
½ tsp • 2.5 mL	freshly ground black pepper
8	long, flat, metal skewers

1 Combine all marinade ingredients in a non-reactive bowl.

2 Cut meat along the grain into long strips, 3 × 6 inches (8 × 15 cm) and ½ inch (1 cm) thick. Pound the meat strips lightly with a wooden mallet.

3 Add meat to marinade and toss gently. Cover and marinate in the refrigerator for up to 24 hours.

4 Make a basting liquid by combining butter, lime juice, salt and pepper.

5 Thread meat strips onto skewers. Grill over high heat for 3–4 minutes per side, turning and basting with basting liquid.

6 Remove cooked kebabs from skewers and serve on *lavash* (see page 229) brushed with basting liquid or over saffron rice pilaf (recipe page 219). Sprinkle with sumac.

MEAT KEBABS

Seekh kabab

SERVES 4

Marinade

½ cup • 125 mL	olive oil
½ cup • 125 mL	lime juice
1	large onion, finely chopped
2 tsp • 10 mL	minced garlic
1 tsp • 5 mL	dried oregano
1 tsp • 5 mL	salt
1 tsp • 5 mL	freshly ground black pepper

Kebabs

2 lb • 1 kg	boneless meat (chicken, lamb or beef) cut into 1½-inch (4-cm) cubes
2 Tbsp • 25 mL	melted clarified butter or ghee
2 Tbsp • 25 mL	lime juice
½ tsp • 2.5 mL	ground saffron dissolved in 2 Tbsp (25 mL) water or milk
½ tsp • 2.5 mL	salt
½ tsp • 2.5 mL	freshly ground black pepper
2	red onions, quartered and layers separated
2	green bell peppers, cut into 1½-inch (4-cm) squares
2	medium tomatoes, each cut into 8 wedges
8	long, thin, flat metal skewers

1 Combine all marinade ingredients in a non-reactive bowl. Add meat cubes and toss well to coat. Cover and marinate for up to 24 hours in the refrigerator.

2 Make a basting liquid by combining butter, lime juice, saffron, salt and pepper.

3 Thread 5–6 pieces of meat alternating with onion, green pepper and tomato onto each skewer.

4 Grill over high heat for 4–5 minutes per side (chicken will take less time), turning and brushing with basting liquid frequently.

5 Remove meat and vegetables from each skewer. Serve over *chelou* (see page 228) or *lavash* (see page 229) brushed with basting liquid. Sprinkle with sumac.

CHICKEN KEBABS

Jujeh kabab

Marinade

1 cup • 250 mL	lime juice
2 Tbsp • 25 mL	olive oil
2	medium onions, thinly sliced
2 tsp • 10 mL	salt
1 tsp • 5 mL	saffron dissolved in 2 Tbsp (25 mL) hot milk

Kebabs

4 lb • 2 kg	chicken, cut into 3–4-inch (8–10-cm) pieces
2 Tbsp • 25 mL	melted clarified butter
2 Tbsp • 25 mL	fresh lime juice
½ tsp • 2.5 mL	salt
½ tsp • 2.5 mL	freshly ground black pepper
8	long, flat metal skewers, ¾ inch (2 cm) wide
2	long, thin metal skewers
4	medium tomatoes, quartered

1 Combine all marinade ingredients in a large non-reactive bowl. Add chicken pieces and mix well to coat. Cover and marinate up to 24 hours in the refrigerator.

2 Make a basting liquid by combining butter, lime juice, salt and pepper.

3 Thread chicken pieces onto the wider skewers and tomato wedges onto thin narrow skewers.

4 Grill chicken skewers over medium heat until the juices run clear, for about 6–8 minutes per side, turning and brushing with basting liquid often. Grill tomatoes for 1–2 minutes, until slightly charred.

5 Serve chicken and tomatoes on *lavash* (see page 229) and garnish with lime wedges and chopped parsley.

Ground MEAT KEBABS

Kabab-e Kubideh

SERVES 4–5

1 lb • 500 g	ground lamb
1 lb • 500 g	ground beef or veal
1 Tbsp • 15 mL	yogurt
2	medium onions, finely chopped or grated
2 tsp • 10 mL	salt
1 tsp • 5 mL	garlic paste
½ tsp • 2.5 mL	freshly ground black pepper
8–10	long, flat, metal skewers, 1-inch (2.5-cm) wide
¼ cup • 50 mL	melted clarified butter
1 tsp • 5 mL	saffron dissolved in 2 Tbsp (30 mL) hot water
	sumac and lime juice for sprinkling

1 Combine lamb and beef and run through a food processor until finely minced. Add yogurt, onion, salt, garlic, pepper and half of dissolved saffron. Knead the meat mixture until well combined. Cover and refrigerate for 4–6 hours or preferably overnight to let flavors to develop.

2 Divide the mixture into 8–10 portions. Moisten hands with water and wrap one portion around each skewer to form a sausage, 5–6 inches (12–15 cm) long. Press the meat all along its length to form ridges at intervals. This will ensure it does not fall off the skewer while cooking.

3 Make a basting liquid by combining butter with remaining dissolved saffron.

4 Remove the cooking grill and suspend skewers directly over the fire, using the edges of the fire box to support the ends of the skewers. Grill over high heat, turning frequently and brushing occasionally with basting liquid to ensure the meat does not become dry.

5 Serve over *lavash* (see page 229) or *sangak* (see page 231) brushed with basting liquid and sprinkled with *sumac* and lime juice.

STURGEON KEBABS
Kabab-e Ozunborun

These kebabs are popular in northern Iran as sturgeon comes from the Caspian Sea. Its firm texture and oily flesh make it ideal for grilling.

Marinade

SERVES 4

1 cup • 250 mL	lime or lemon juice
1	large onion, finely chopped or grated
1 tsp • 5 mL	salt
½ tsp • 2.5 mL	freshly ground black pepper

Kebabs

2 lb • 1 kg	sturgeon fillets, cut into 1½-inch (4-cm) pieces
½ cup • 125 mL	lime juice
¼ cup • 50 mL	melted clarified butter
1 Tbsp • 15 mL	tomato paste
8	long, flat, metal skewers, ¾-inch (2-cm) wide

1 Mix lime or lemon juice, onion, salt and pepper in a non-reactive bowl. Add fish and toss gently to coat. Cover and marinate for 2–4 hours in the refrigerator.

2 Thread 5–6 pieces of fish onto each skewer. Prepare basting sauce by bringing lime juice, clarified butter, and tomato paste to a boil in a pan and simmering for 5 minutes.

3 Grill fish over medium heat for 4–5 minutes, turning and brushing with basting sauce.

4 Serve with rice pilaf, garnished with slices of lemon or lime and chopped parsley.

Spicy BEEF KEBABS
Pasanda Kabab

SERVES 4

Marinade

1 cup • 250 mL	yogurt
¼ cup • 50 mL	lemon juice
2 tsp • 10 mL	garlic paste
2 tsp • 10 mL	ginger paste
2 tsp • 10 mL	dried mustard
1 tsp • 5 mL	garam masala (recipe page 227)
1 tsp • 5 mL	ground green cardamom
1 tsp • 5 mL	salt
1 tsp • 5 mL	red chili powder

Kebabs

2 lb • 1 kg	boneless beef sirloin cut into 1½-inch (4-cm) pieces
8	long metal skewers
¼ cup • 50 mL	melted butter for basting

1   Combine all marinade ingredients in a non-reactive bowl. With a wooden mallet, pound each piece of beef slightly to flatten. Add beef to marinade and toss well to coat. Cover and marinate overnight in the refrigerator.

2   Remove beef from marinade and bring to room temperature. Thread 5–6 pieces onto each skewer, leaving a small space between each piece.

3   Grill skewers over medium-high heat for 8–10 minutes, turning frequently and basting with butter occasionally.

4   Slide kebabs off the skewers and sprinkle with salt, black pepper and garam masala. Serve with rice pilaf or onion, tomato and lettuce salad.

Ground BEEF or LAMB KEBABS

Seekh Kababs

2 lb • 1 kg	ground lean beef or ground lamb
1	medium onion, finely chopped or grated
¼ cup • 50 mL	finely chopped fresh mint
¼ cup • 50 mL	finely chopped fresh cilantro
1	egg, beaten
1 Tbsp • 15 mL	ginger paste
1 Tbsp • 15 mL	garlic paste
1 Tbsp • 15 mL	lemon juice
2 tsp • 10 mL	ground cumin
1 tsp • 5 mL	garam masala (recipe page 227)
1 tsp • 5 mL	red chili powder
1 tsp • 5 mL	ground black pepper
1½ tsp • 7.5 mL	salt
8	long iron skewers (4-sided)
¼ cup • 50 mL	melted butter for basting

1 Mix together all the kebab ingredients except the melted butter in a non-reactive bowl. Knead to mix thoroughly. Cover and refrigerate overnight to develop flavors.

2 Divide meat mixture into 8 portions. Moisten hands with water and wrap each portion around a skewer to form a long sausage-like shape, about 8–10 inches (20–30 cm) long and 1 inch (2.5 cm) in diameter. Keep hands wet to help form the perfect shape around the skewers.

3 Remove cooking grill and suspend skewers directly over the fire with the ends resting on the edges of the fire box. Grill over high heat for 8–10 minutes, turning skewers frequently and basting with melted butter occasionally.

4 Remove cooked kebabs from skewers and serve with onion slices, mint chutney and naan.

MUTTON KEBABS

Barra kabob

SERVES 6 ## Marinade

¼ cup • 50 mL	wine vinegar
3	medium onions, grated
1 tsp • 5 mL	ground coriander
1 tsp • 5 mL	salt
1 tsp • 5 mL	freshly ground black pepper

Kebabs

2 lb • 1 kg	boneless lean lamb or sheep meat, cut into 1½-inch (4-cm) pieces
¼ lb • 125 g	mutton fat, cut into 1-inch (2.5-cm) cubes
12	long metal skewers

1 Mix all marinade ingredients in a non-reactive bowl. Add meat and toss well to coat each piece thoroughly. Cover and marinate in the refrigerator overnight.

2 Thread 4–5 pieces of meat alternating with mutton fat onto each skewer.

3 Grill over medium heat, turning frequently to ensure fat melts and the meat is evenly brown on all sides, about 10–12 minutes.

4 Serve with tomato, radish and cucumber salad.

Ground LAMB KEBABS

Kiyma kabob

2 lb • 1 kg	**double-ground lamb**
3	**medium onions, finely chopped**
1 tsp • 5 mL	**salt**
½ tsp • 2.5 mL	**cayenne pepper**
1	**beaten egg**
8	**long metal skewers**
¼ cup • 50 mL	**all-purpose flour**

1 Mix ground lamb with onion, salt, pepper and egg. Knead well to ensure everything is well mixed.

2 Divide mixture into 8 portions. Moisten hands with water and wrap each portion around a skewer to form a long sausage about 1 inch (2.5 cm) in diameter. Dust each skewer with flour.

3 Remove grill and suspend skewers directly over fire with their ends resting on the edges of the fire box. Grill over high heat for 5–6 minutes, turning constantly until evenly brown on all sides.

4 Serve with onion and tomato salad.

Laos

Thailand

Vietnam

Cambodia

Philippines

Brunei

Malaysia

Singapore

(Borneo)

Indonesia

(Sumatra)

Southeast Asia

The countries of Southeast Asia are Brunei, Cambodia, Indonesia, Laos, Malaysia, the Philippines, Singapore, Thailand and Vietnam. Their cuisines have been greatly influenced by China and India for centuries, and that persists even today. The Chinese introduced stir-frying and the use of soy sauce, noodles and soybean products. From India came an array of spices for flavoring curries. Furthermore, most Southeast Asian countries are home to sizable Chinese and Indian migrant populations that have influenced the local food scene with their own cuisines. Other colonial powers such as the Dutch, British, French and Portuguese also left their mark on the region, but to a lesser extent. The resulting fusion, enriched with local herbs, condiments and sauces, has produced distinctive cuisines in each country. Despite this, there are common threads that link them all: the use of coconut milk, lemon grass, galangal, lime and lime leaves, chilies, shrimp paste and fish sauce.

Malacca and Java in Indonesia dominated the spice trade; the exotic spices attracted hordes of traders from China, India and Arabia, followed by Portuguese and Dutch explorers. It is widely held that Arab and Indian Muslim traders in Java first introduced kebab cookery, from which satay cooking evolved. From Indonesia, it spread to Malaysia, Singapore, Thailand, Vietnam and Cambodia. Although both Malaysia and Thailand lay claim to inventing satays, historical records indicate that they were derivatives of regular kebabs introduced initially in Java by Muslim spice traders.

Kebab cookery in Southeast Asia is characterized by two significant changes. First, the traditional metal skewer gave way to the bamboo skewer, which is almost universally used in this region. Second, the size of the meat threaded onto skewers became much smaller, thus considerably reducing the cooking time. Throughout Southeast Asia, satay, or *sate*, in the form of delicious bite-size pieces of meat strung onto a bamboo skewer and grilled over a long, narrow charcoal brazier are sold on the street and served with a sweet dipping sauce, usually made of ground peanuts, spices and coconut milk. They vary from stall to stall and from region to region throughout Southeast Asia and can be had at any time of day or night as an inexpensive snack, appetizer or main meal. Satays are also found in the most sophisticated restaurants of Bangkok, Jakarta, Kuala Lumpur and Singapore.

Indonesia occupies the world's largest archipelago, with over 13,000 islands. It emerged from

Japanese and Dutch occupation to become an independent nation in 1949. Today this country of over 200 million inhabitants is a vibrant mixture of ethnicities and cultures enriched by interactions not only with its immediate neighbors but also with China, India, Africa, the Middle East and Europe. Long before the Dutch colonized Indonesia, the Spanish, Portuguese, Chinese, Indians and Arabs had established strong cultural and trade ties with Java and Sumatra, and a few chose to settle down in these islands. Indonesian food varies from one region to another and reflects many influences, but rice, coconut milk, lemon grass, galangal and tamarind and spices like coriander, pepper and turmeric are central to all Indonesian cuisine. All kinds of meats are consumed in this predominantly Muslim country, but the use of pork is limited to areas where non-Muslim minorities live. In west Sumatra, known for its Padang style of cooking, the food tends to be very spicy. In Java, grilled and steamed seafood is popular and in Bali, the only part of Indonesia with a predominantly Hindu population, the cooking style is distinctive and pork dishes are available.

Satay is referred to as *sateh* in the Indonesian language, Bahasa Indonesia. The variety of satays is huge; each island seems to have its own distinctive seasonings, marinades, dipping sauces and way of cooking satays and there are regional variations within each island. Javanese marinades are quite mild, consisting mostly of ginger, garlic, soy sauce, lemon juice, coconut milk, chilies and *ketjap manis* (Indonesian sweet sauce). In Sumatra, particularly west Sumatra, known for its hot and spicy Padang style of foods, beef is the preferred meat and *sateh padang* (spicy beef) is very popular. The island of Sulwesi is known for its *sateh makassar* (beef) and *sateh babi pedis* (spicy pork). Balinese culture and cuisine tend to be distinctive and not seen in other parts of Indonesia. Balinese food tends to be spicy hot and aromatic. It is richer than that of the rest of Indonesia.

Of all the countries in Southeast Asia, Thailand is the only nation that escaped colonization, and its cuisine evolved harmoniously from Chinese, Indian, Indonesian, Malaysian and Buddhist influences. As a Buddhist country, animals were not killed for food and a tradition of vegetarian food developed. However, with the passage of time and increasing interactions with other cultures, small amounts of meat, fish and shellfish were incorporated into Thai food. Today it has evolved into a spicy, pungent cuisine moderated by the addition of coconut milk, locally grown herbs and other ingredients, such as lime, lemon grass, basil, galangal, ginger and fresh cilantro. Pork, poultry, beef and seafood are now used but in relatively small amounts augmented by larger quantities of vegetables and rice.

Satays are popular Thai street food and carts and stalls are a common sight in the lanes and alleys of Bangkok and other cities. The satays are served with a peanut sauce and cucumber slices drizzled with a sweet and sour Thai dressing called *nam thaeng kwa* (see page 230). Besides satays, a variety of grilled skewered foods, such as shrimp balls, fish balls, sausages, whole squids and other seafood are sold from street stalls throughout Thailand.

Malaysian and Singaporean cuisine is greatly influenced by the Malays, Chinese, Indians and Portuguese who settled this region. Malaysian food without seasoning is unthinkable; cumin, pepper, coriander, cardamom, turmeric, star anise, chilies, lemon grass, pandan leaf, kaffir lime, basil and galangal are common ingredients. Meats include mutton, beef and chicken. Pork is not used among the predominantly Muslim population but it is a preferred meat for the Chinese population in Malaysia and Singapore. Satays in Malaysia and Singapore tend to be spicier than those in other Southeast Asian countries. A satay is at least partially defined by the peanut sauce it is served with. Malaysian sauce is rich, spicy and pleasantly nutty, whereas Chinese-style sauce, served with pork satays, is thick, smooth and made from sweet potatoes and chilies.

Vietnamese cuisine is highly influenced by its northern neighbor China, particularly in North Vietnam, although Indian, Cambodian, Laotian and Thai influences are seen in the use of spices and curries in the south of the country. Vietnam was a French colony from 1895 until 1954 and some French influence persists even today in the form of pâtés, wine-based cooking, French bread, coffee and the rich sauces served in some upscale restaurants. Vietnamese cuisine is characterized by its delicate balance of flavors, textures and colors. Beef, chicken, duck and seafood are consumed in small quantities, augmented by fresh vegetables, herbs, noodles and fruits. Dishes tend to be light, mostly seafood oriented, with a generous use of fresh herbs like mint, cilantro, lemon grass, lime and basil. Most Vietnamese dishes are served with the ubiquitous all-purpose salty-sour fish sauce called *nuoc mam* or a spicy dipping sauce called *nuoc cham* (see page 230). Grilling is quite popular throughout Vietnam and the marinades for satays or brochettes generally do not use much oil.

Although Laotian and Cambodian cuisine uses similar herbs and spices to those used in Thai cooking, it tends to be less fiery. There is a decided preference for marine and freshwater fish and seafood, and although beef, pork and chicken are eaten, meat is used in small quantities as a condiment, rather than as a main dish. Rice is a staple in both countries but Laotians prefer sticky rice and, because both countries experienced French colonial rule, French-style baguettes often compete with rice as the carbohydrate of choice. Pork, beef and prawn satays in these countries are similar to Thai satays.

Of all the Southeast Asian countries, the Philippines remains the only one where kebab or satay cookery has not made significant inroads. Although skewered meat is sold by vendors from their carts in Manila's local markets and streets, it is not widespread in other parts of the country. Local kebab-like preparations of beef, chicken, pork and fish, known as *inihaw na manok* (chicken), *inihaw na baka* (beef), *inihaw na baboy* (pork) and *inihaw na isda* (fish) are generally not marinated, but a sauce made of sugar, soy sauce, garlic and black pepper is applied during and after grilling.

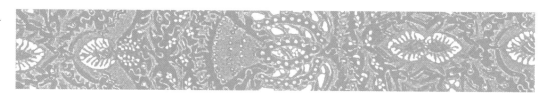

SKEWERED PORK

Saik Chrouk Ch'ranouitk

SERVES 4

Marinade

4	shallots
1-inch • 2.5-cm	piece of *galangal* (see page 228) or fresh ginger
2	fresh red chilies, seeded
2	cloves garlic
2	stalks lemon grass, white part only, sliced
2 Tbsp • 25 mL	fish sauce
2 Tbsp • 25 mL	coconut milk
1 Tbsp • 15 mL	sugar
1 tsp • 5 mL	turmeric
½ cup • 125 mL	shredded unsweetened coconut

Kebabs

1 lb • 500 g	lean pork, cut into strips 3 inches (7 cm) long, 1 inch (2.5 cm) wide and ¼ inch (0.5 cm) thick
12	medium presoaked bamboo skewers
2 Tbsp • 25 mL	vegetable oil or melted butter for basting

1 In a food processor blend all marinade ingredients except shredded coconut to obtain a thin paste. Transfer paste to a bowl and mix in the coconut.

2 Pour paste over pork and toss well to coat. Cover and marinate in the refrigerator overnight.

3 Thread one or two pork strips onto each skewer. Grill over medium heat for 2–3 minutes per side, turning once and basting with oil or butter.

4 Serve immediately with a dipping sauce of your choice.

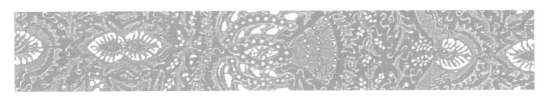

Grilled BEEF SKEWERS
Saiko Ang Kroeung

Marinade

1	stalk lemon grass, sliced, white part only
1-inch • 2.5 cm	piece of galangal
¼ cup • 50 mL	fish sauce *(nuoc nam)* (see page 230)
2	cloves garlic
1	red chili, seeded
2	kaffir lime leaves (see page 229)
2 Tbsp • 25 mL	vegetable oil
1 Tbsp • 15 mL	lime juice
½ tsp • 2.5 mL	freshly ground black pepper

Kebabs

1 lb • 500 g	beefsteak, cut into strips 4 inches (10 cm) long, 1 inch (2.5 cm) wide, and ¼ inch (0.5 cm) thick
12	medium presoaked bamboo skewers

1 In a food processor, blend all marinade ingredients to a purée. Transfer the purée to a bowl, add beef strips and toss gently to coat. Cover and marinate at room temperature for at least 30 minutes or up to 4 hours in the refrigerator.

2 Remove meat and reserve marinade. Thread each strip onto a skewer.

3 Grill skewers over high heat for about 2 minutes per side, brushing with marinade at each turn.

4 Serve immediately with a dipping sauce of your choice.

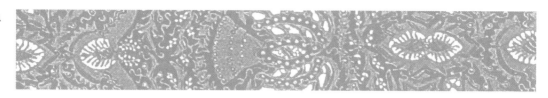

MINCED FISH SATAY

Sateh Pusut Ikan

SERVES 8

2 lb • 1 kg	firm white fish fillet
1 Tbsp • 15 mL	chopped cilantro
2 Tbsp • 25 mL	chopped green onion
1	egg white
1	medium onion, chopped
2 Tbsp • 25 mL	lemon juice
2 Tbsp • 25 mL	vegetable oil
1 Tbsp • 15 mL	sliced lemon grass (white part)
1 Tbsp • 15 mL	fish sauce
1 tsp • 5 mL	sugar
1 tsp • 5 mL	chopped kaffir lime leaves (see page 229)
1 tsp • 5 mL	shrimp paste
1 tsp • 5 mL	garlic paste
½ tsp • 2.5 mL	turmeric
½ tsp • 2.5 mL	ground cinnamon
½ tsp • 2.5 mL	salt
½ tsp • 2.5 mL	ground black pepper
¼ tsp • 1 mL	ground nutmeg
¼ tsp • 1 mL	ground clove
several	lemon grass stalks, cut into 6-inch (15-cm) lengths as skewers
¼ cup • 50 mL	vegetable oil mixed with equal amount of water for basting

1 In a food processor, coarsely grind fish, cilantro, green onion and egg white. Set aside.

2 Purée the remaining ingredients (except lemon grass stalks and ¼ cup/50 mL oil) in the food processor. Transfer the contents to a large bowl. Add minced fish mixture and mix well. Cover and refrigerate overnight to allow flavors to develop.

3 Moisten hands with water and roll fish mixture into small balls about the size of an egg. Push a lemon grass stalk through each fish ball, then squeeze the mixture gently to form a sausage around the stalk. Make as many skewers as the fish mixture will permit.

4 Grill over high heat for 4–6 minutes, turning frequently and basting with oil and water mixture occasionally.

5 Serve with satay or a dipping sauce of your choice.

• *This specialty of Bali uses lemon grass stalks as skewers. However, if lemon grass is not available, medium presoaked bamboo skewers can be substituted.*

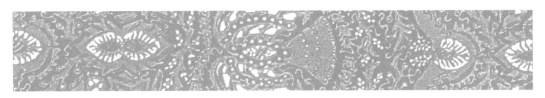

Minced fish and PRAWN SATAY
Sateh Lilit

Balinese Spice Paste

10	shallots
4	candlenuts
4–6	green chilies, seeded
1 Tbsp • 15 mL	chopped garlic
1 Tbsp • 15 mL	chopped ginger
1 Tbsp • 15 mL	tomato paste
2 tsp • 10 mL	ground coriander
1 tsp • 5 mL	turmeric

Kebabs

1 lb • 500 g	fresh snapper fillet
1 lb • 500 g	fresh raw shrimps, peeled
2 cups • 500 mL	freshly grated or dried coconut
3 Tbsp • 45 mL	brown sugar
1 Tbsp • 15 mL	finely chopped kaffir lime leaves (see page 229)
1 Tbsp • 15 mL	freshly ground black pepper
2 tsp • 10 mL	salt
several	green lemon grass stalks, cut into 6-inch (15-cm) lengths as skewers

1 Process all spice paste ingredients in a food processor or blender. You will have approximately ½ cup (125 mL). Transfer the paste to a jar and store in the refrigerator until needed.

2 In a food processor, finely mince snapper fillets and shrimps. Gradually add spice paste, coconut, sugar, lime leaves, pepper and salt. Continue running the food processor to obtain a thick mixture.

3 Moisten hands with water and wrap about 1 Tbsp (15 mL) of mixture around one end of each lemon grass stalk in the form of a small sausage. Make as many skewers as the fish-prawn mixture will permit.

4 Grill over medium heat for 4–6 minutes, turning frequently until golden brown on all sides.

5 Serve as an appetizer, with or without dipping sauce.

• *This exotic Balinese satay is reputed to be the most delicious of the Indonesian satays and uses fresh lemon grass stalks as skewers. These are traditionally grilled over a fire of coconut husk.*

• *A candlenut is a tropical nut that is hard and high in fat; it can be found in stores that sell Southeast Asian foods.*

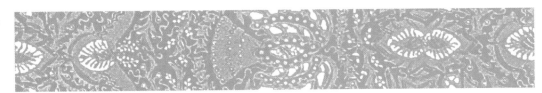

CHICKEN SATAY

Sateh Ayam

SERVES 8

2	**medium onions, coarsely chopped**
1 inch • 2.5 cm	**piece ginger**
2 Tbsp • 25 mL	**light soy sauce**
2 Tbsp • 25 mL	**lemon juice**
2 Tbsp • 25 mL	**palm sugar**
1 tsp • 5 mL	**salt**
1 Tbsp • 15 mL	**sesame oil**
1 tsp • 5 mL	***sambal oelek* (see page 231) or 2 seeded red chilies**
1 tsp • 5 mL	**ground coriander**
½ tsp • 2.5 mL	**turmeric**
2 lb • 1 kg	**boneless chicken breasts or thighs, cut into 1-inch (2.5-cm) pieces**
15–20	**medium presoaked bamboo skewers**
¼ cup • 50 mL	**oil mixed with equal amount of water for basting**
½ cup • 125 mL	**coconut milk**

1 In a food processor, blend onions, ginger, soy sauce, lemon juice, sugar, salt, oil, sambal oelek, coriander and turmeric to obtain a paste. Transfer to a non-reactive bowl, add chicken pieces and toss well to coat. Cover and refrigerate overnight.

2 Remove chicken pieces and reserve marinade. Thread 3–4 pieces of chicken onto each skewer.

3 Grill over medium heat for 5–6 minutes, turning and basting with oil-water mixture frequently.

4 Transfer reserved marinade to a pan and add coconut milk. Bring to a boil, and then simmer for 5 minutes, stirring constantly. Serve as a dipping sauce with satays.

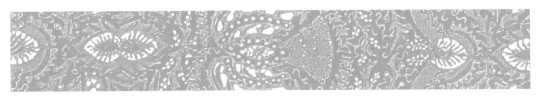

PORK SATAY
Sateh Babi Manis

4	**shallots, finely minced**
2	**red chilies, seeded and finely chopped**
3 Tbsp • 45 mL	*ketjap manis* **(see page 229)**
1 Tbsp • 15 mL	**lemon juice**
1 tsp • 5 mL	**ginger paste**
1 tsp • 5 mL	**garlic paste**
1 tsp • 5 mL	**ground coriander**
1 tsp • 5 mL	**salt**
½ tsp • 2.5 mL	**turmeric**
½ tsp • 2.5 mL	**white pepper**
2 lb • 1 kg	**lean pork cut into 1-inch (2.5-cm) pieces**
16	**medium presoaked bamboo skewers**
2 Tbsp • 25 mL	**melted butter mixed with 2 Tbsp (25 mL) lemon juice for basting**

1   Combine shallots, chilies, ketjap manis, lemon juice, ginger, garlic, coriander, salt, turmeric and pepper in a large non-reactive bowl. Add pork and toss well to coat. Cover and marinate in the refrigerator overnight.

2   Remove pork pieces from marinade. Thread 4 pieces onto each skewer.

3   Grill skewers over medium heat for 2–3 minutes per side, turning and basting with butter and lemon mixture frequently.

4   Serve with *sambal kecap* (see page 231).

•   *In Bali* sateh babi *(pork) and* sateh penyu *(turtle meat) are the most popular choices.* Sateh penyu, *made of chopped green sea turtle meat mixed with spices, is a highly appreciated delicacy and serving it to guests is regarded as a sign of wealth and prestige.*

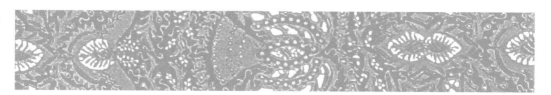

LAMB SATAY

Sateh Kambing Madura

SERVES 4

1	small onion, coarsely chopped
2 Tbsp • 25 mL	*ketjap manis* (see page 229)
2 Tbsp • 25 mL	lime juice
2 Tbsp • 25 mL	soy sauce
1 tsp • 5 mL	*sambal oelek* (see page 231) or 2 red chilies, seeded
1 tsp • 5 mL	garlic paste
1 tsp • 5 mL	ginger paste
½ tsp • 2.5 mL	shrimp paste
½ tsp • 2.5 mL	ground black pepper
½ tsp • 2.5 mL	ground cumin
2 Tbsp • 25 mL	grated fresh or dried coconut
1 lb • 500 g	lean boneless lamb, cut into 1 inch (2.5 cm) cubes
8	medium presoaked bamboo skewers
¼ cup • 50 mL	coconut milk for basting

1 In a food processor, blend onion, *ketjap manis*, lime juice, soy sauce, *sambal oelek*, garlic, ginger, shrimp paste, pepper and cumin to a paste. Transfer to a non-reactive bowl, mix in grated coconut and add lamb cubes. Toss well to coat. Cover and marinate overnight in the refrigerator.

2 Thread 4 lamb pieces onto each skewer and bring the meat to room temperature.

3 Grill over medium-high heat for 3–4 minutes per side, turning and basting with coconut milk frequently, until slightly charred.

4 Serve with *sambal ketjap* (see page 231) as a dipping sauce and garnish with fried onions.

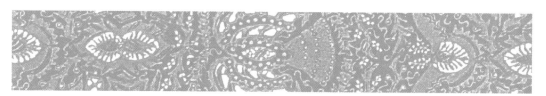

CHICKEN SATAY
Satay Ayam

Marinade

2	medium onions or 4 shallots
4	cloves garlic
1 Tbsp • 15 mL	chopped lemon grass, white part only
2 Tbsp • 25 mL	sugar
2 Tbsp • 25 mL	vegetable oil
2 tsp • 10 mL	ground coriander
1 tsp • 5 mL	ground cumin
1 tsp • 5 mL	turmeric
1 tsp • 5 mL	salt
½ tsp • 2.5 mL	chili powder

Kebabs

2 lb • 1 kg	boneless chicken breast or thigh, sliced ¼ inch (0.5 cm) thick, 2 inches (5 cm) long and 1 inch (2.5 cm) wide
16–20	medium presoaked bamboo skewers
¼ cup • 50 mL	oil mixed with equal amount of water for basting

1 Blend onion, garlic, oil and lemon grass in a food processor. Transfer the paste to a non-reactive bowl. Add remaining marinade ingredients and mix well.

2 Add chicken pieces and toss well to coat. Cover and marinate in the refrigerator for no more than 6 hours. Thread 3–4 pieces onto each skewer.

3 Grill satays over medium-high heat for 2–3 minutes, turning and basting with oil-water mixture frequently until meat is slightly charred.

4 Serve satays with peanut sauce, slices of onion, cucumber and packets of compressed rice, *ketupat* (see page 229), if available.

• *Satay ayam is an all-time favorite throughout Malaysia. This recipe is from my friend Ben Ho, who first introduced me to the fine art of satay cooking. The marinade can also be used for beef.*

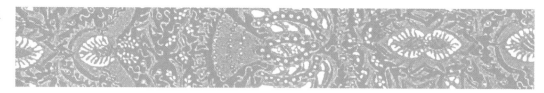

BEEF SATAY
Satay Daging

Marinade

2 Tbsp • 25 mL	light soy sauce
1 Tbsp • 15 mL	lemon juice
1 Tbsp • 15 mL	finely chopped shallots
1 Tbsp • 15 mL	palm sugar
1 Tbsp • 15 mL	vegetable oil
1 Tbsp • 15 mL	ground coriander
1 Tbsp • 15 mL	ground cumin
1 tsp • 5 mL	garlic paste
1 tsp • 5 mL	ginger paste
½ tsp • 2.5 mL	salt
½ tsp • 2.5 mL	chili powder

Kebabs

2 lb • 1 kg	boneless top sirloin steak, cut into pieces, 1 inch (2.5 cm) long and ½ inch (1 cm) thick
16–20	medium presoaked bamboo skewers

1 Mix all marinade ingredients in a non-reactive bowl. Add beef and toss well to coat. Cover and marinate overnight in the refrigerator.

2 Remove meat and reserve marinade. Thread 3–4 pieces of beef onto each skewer.

3 Grill over high heat for 2–3 minutes per side, turning and basting with reserved marinade frequently.

4 Serve with peanut sauce (recipe page 220), *ketupat* (see page 229) if available, red onion slices and cucumber.

CHICKEN TIKKA KEBABS   page 116

CHICKEN AND PORK SATAY   pages 149, 150

SHRIMP LOLLIPOPS   page 156

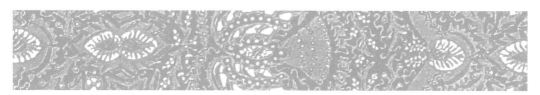

CHICKEN or BEEF SATAY

Satay Kajang

Marinade

8	shallots, chopped
1	stalk lemon grass (white part only), sliced
2 Tbsp • 25 mL	vegetable oil
2 Tbsp • 25 mL	sugar
1 Tbsp • 15 mL	roasted peanuts
1 tsp • 5 mL	ground cumin
1 tsp • 5 mL	ground coriander
1 tsp • 5 mL	turmeric
1 tsp • 5 mL	salt
½ tsp • 2.5 mL	ground cinnamon

Kebabs

2 lb • 1 kg	boneless chicken or beef cut into pieces ¼ inch (0.5 cm) thick and 1½ inches (4 cm) long
16–20	medium presoaked bamboo skewers
¼ cup • 50 mL	coconut milk mixed with an equal amount of oil for basting

1 Purée all marinade ingredients in blender. Transfer to a non-reactive bowl. Add the chicken or beef pieces and toss well to coat. Cover and marinate in the refrigerator overnight.

2 Remove meat and thread about 3 pieces onto each skewer.

3 Grill over medium heat for 5–7 minutes, turning and basting with coconut milk and oil mixture frequently. This helps keep meat from drying out and adds flavor.

4 Serve with peanut sauce (recipe page 220), sliced cucumber and sliced red onions.

- *In Malaysia, some satays are known to be particularly tasty and are named after the places where they originated. For example, this satay is from Kajang near Kuala Lumpur. It is often said that if you want the absolute best in satay, you must come to Kajang.*

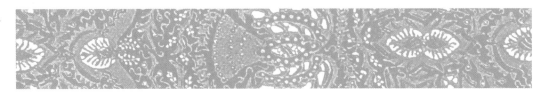

MUTTON SATAY

Satay Kambing

Marinade

3	shallots, finely chopped
2	lemon grass stalks (white part only), finely sliced
1 Tbsp • 15 mL	vegetable oil
1 Tbsp • 15 mL	sugar
1 tsp • 5 mL	ginger paste
1 tsp • 5 mL	garlic paste
1 tsp • 5 mL	ground coriander
1 tsp • 5 mL	ground cumin
1 tsp • 5 mL	ground fennel
½ tsp • 2.5 mL	turmeric
½ tsp • 2.5 mL	salt
½ tsp • 2.5 mL	chili powder

Kebabs

1 lb • 500 g	lamb or goat meat cut into pieces 1½ inches (4 cm) long and ¼ inch (0.5 cm) thick
8	medium presoaked bamboo skewers
¼ cup • 50 mL	coconut milk mixed with an equal amount of oil for basting

1 Combine all marinade ingredients in a non-reactive bowl. Add meat and toss well to coat. Cover and marinate for at least 6 hours and preferably overnight in the refrigerator.

2 Thread 3–4 pieces of meat onto each skewer. Grill skewers over medium heat for about 3 minutes per side, turning and basting with coconut milk and oil mixture frequently. The meat should be slightly charred on the outside.

3 Serve with peanut sauce (recipe page 220), sliced cucumber and onion.

• *Another much sought-after satay is Johor Satay Kambing from Johor Bahru near Singapore.*

• *An interesting variation of skewered foods is found in Lok Lok stalls in Penang, where a variety of seafood, such as whole prawns, cuttlefish, squids, fish slices, jellyfish, fish and shrimp balls are skewered onto bamboo sticks and boiled in water for varying lengths of time. These sticks are dipped in a rich nutty sauce before serving and the skewer ends are color-coded to indicate the price of each stick.*

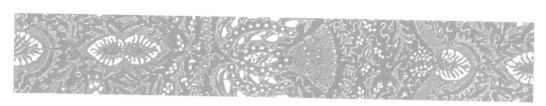

Nonya Style PORK SATAY

Marinade

½ cup • 125 mL	coconut milk
2 Tbsp • 25 mL	soy sauce
3	shallots
2 tsp • 10 mL	five-spice powder
1 tsp • 5 mL	garlic paste
1 tsp • 5 mL	ginger paste
1 tsp • 5 mL	ground Szechwan pepper
1 tsp • 5 mL	roasted ground coriander
1 tsp • 5 mL	roasted ground cumin

Kebabs

2 lb • 1 kg	pork tenderloin cut into strips 3–4 inches (7–10 cm) long, ½ inch (1 cm) thick, and 1 inch (2.5 cm) wide
16	medium presoaked bamboo skewers
¼ cup • 50 mL	oil mixed with an equal amount of water for basting

1 Combine all marinade ingredients in an electric blender. Purée, then transfer to a non-reactive bowl. Add pork strips and toss well to coat. Cover and marinate for at least 4 hours or overnight in the refrigerator.

2 Remove meat from marinade and thread one strip onto each skewer. Let stand to reach room temperature.

3 Grill over medium heat for 3–4 minutes per side, turning and basting with oil and water mixture frequently.

4 Serve with peanut sauce of your choice, sliced cucumber and red onion, and *ketupat* (see page 229), if available.

- *This satay is a popular street food with the non-Muslim Chinese population of Singapore.*

- *The Nonya cuisine of Malaysia and Singapore is spicy-hot and incorporates four culinary cultures —Chinese, Malay, Indian and Indonesian.*

- *In Singapore and Malaysia, satays are served with slices of raw onion, cucumber and small cakes of compressed glutinous rice, called ketupat, wrapped in tiny woven baskets of coconut leaves.*

- *To make roasted spices, toast the whole spices in a dry frying pan over medium heat until fragrant. Be careful not to burn them. Cool, grind to a powder and store in an airtight container.*

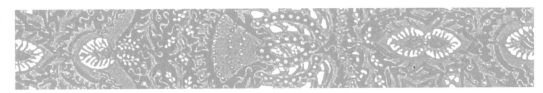

BEEF SATAY

SERVES 8

Marinade

2	medium onions, finely chopped
1	stalk lemon grass (white part), finely chopped
2 Tbsp • 25 mL	soy sauce
2 Tbsp • 25 mL	lemon juice
2 Tbsp • 25 mL	vegetable oil
1 tsp • 5 mL	garlic paste
1 tsp • 5 mL	ground coriander
1 tsp • 5 mL	ground cumin
1 tsp • 5 mL	ground turmeric

Kebabs

2 lb • 1 kg	lean beef, sliced into strips 2 inches (5 cm) long, 1 inch (2.5 cm) wide and ¼ inch (0.5 cm) thick
2 Tbsp • 25 mL	brown sugar
16	medium presoaked bamboo skewers
¼ cup • 25 mL	oil mixed with an equal amount of water for basting

1 Combine all marinade ingredients except sugar in a non-reactive bowl. Add beef strips and toss well to coat. Cover and marinate for 6–8 hours or overnight in the refrigerator.

2 Remove beef from marinade and discard marinade. Toss beef add brown sugar to mix and marinate for a further 4–6 hours. Do not marinate longer because sugar acts as a tenderizer and if marinated too long lean beef will become mushy. Thread 2–3 pieces onto each skewer.

3 Grill over high heat for 2–3 minutes per side, turning and basting with oil and water mixture frequently.

4 Serve with peanut sauce (recipe page 220), sliced cucumber and onion.

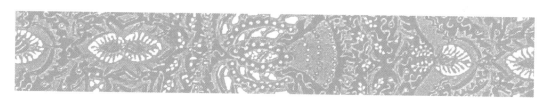

CHICKEN SATAY

Satay Kai Panang

Marinade

1½ cups • 375 mL	**coconut milk**
¼ cup • 50 mL	**vegetable oil**
4	**shallots**
6	**garlic cloves**
1-inch • 2.5-cm	**piece galangal (see page 228)**
1	**stalk lemon grass (tender white part only)**
3 Tbsp • 45 mL	**brown sugar or palm sugar**
3 Tbsp • 45 mL	**Thai fish sauce**
3 Tbsp • 45 mL	**Panang curry paste**
2 Tbsp • 30 mL	**chopped cilantro stems**

Kebabs

2 lb • 1 kg	**boneless chicken breast, cut into long thin strips, ¼ inch (0.5 cm) thick and 1 inch (2.5 cm) wide**
16	**medium presoaked bamboo skewers**

1 In a food processor, blend all marinade ingredients. Transfer the contents to a large non-reactive bowl. Add chicken strips and toss gently to coat. Cover and marinate in the refrigerator overnight.

2 Strain marinade and reserve. Thread one chicken strip along the length of each skewer.

3 Bring reserved marinade to a boil in a saucepan, boil for 2 minutes, remove from heat and set aside.

4 Grill skewers over medium heat for 6–8 minutes, turning often to brown evenly on all sides.

5 Serve with hot marinade sauce.

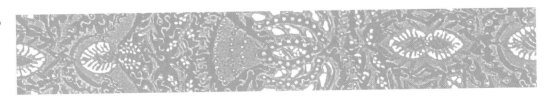

PORK SATAY
Satay Moo

SERVES 8

Marinade

¾ cup • 175 mL	coconut milk
1	stalk lemon grass (white tender part only), sliced
1 inch • 2.5-cm	piece galangal (see page 228)
1 Tbsp • 15 mL	fish sauce
1 Tbsp • 15 mL	palm sugar
2 tsp • 10 mL	ground coriander
2 tsp • 10 mL	ground cumin
1 tsp • 5 mL	turmeric
1 tsp • 5 mL	cayenne pepper
1½ tsp • 7.5 mL	salt

Kebabs

2 lb • 1 kg	lean pork cut into strips 4 inches (10 cm) long, 1 inch (2.5) wide and ¼ inch (0.5 cm) thick
16	medium presoaked bamboo skewers

1 In a food processor, blend all marinade ingredients. Transfer the purée to a large non-reactive bowl, add pork strips and toss gently to coat. Cover and marinate in the refrigerator for at least 4 hours or preferably overnight.

2 Remove meat, reserving marinade. Thread one strip lengthwise onto each skewer.

3 Grill skewers over medium-high heat for 3–4 minutes per side, turning and basting with reserved marinade.

4 Serve with peanut sauce (recipe page 220) and fresh cucumber pickle *ajad* (see page 228).

• *In Thailand street vendors serve this satay with a fiery dipping sauce, and the final bill is settled by counting the number of bamboo skewers on each plate.*

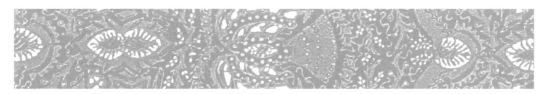

BEEF SATAY
Satay Neua

Marinade

1 cup • 250 mL	**coconut milk**
2 Tbsp • 25 mL	**red curry paste**
2 Tbsp • 25 mL	**brown sugar**
2 Tbsp • 25 mL	**lime juice**
2 Tbsp • 25 mL	**fish sauce**

Kebabs

1 lb • 500 g	**lean beef cut into strips 2½ inches (6.5 cm) long, 1 inch (2.5 cm) wide and ⅛ inch (0.3 cm) thick**
12	**long presoaked bamboo skewers**
¼ cup • 50 mL	**thin coconut milk for basting**

1 Mix all marinade ingredients in a non-reactive bowl. Add meat strips and toss gently to coat. Cover and marinate for at least 4 hours or preferably overnight in the refrigerator.

2 Remove meat from marinade; thread 2 strips onto each skewer.

3 Grill over medium-high heat for 2–3 minutes per side, turning only once and basting with coconut milk.

4 Serve with peanut sauce or Thai cucumber relish *nam thaeng kwa* (see page 230).

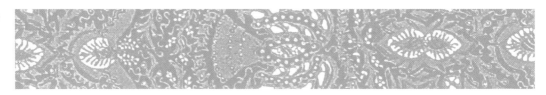

SHRIMP SATAY

Satay Kung

SERVES 8 AS AN APPETIZER

Marinade

2 Tbsp • 25 mL	fish sauce
1 Tbsp • 15 mL	vegetable oil
1 Tbsp • 15 mL	lime juice
1 Tbsp • 15 mL	finely chopped cilantro
1 tsp • 5 mL	garlic paste
1 tsp • 5 mL	ginger paste
1 tsp • 5 mL	sugar
½ tsp • 2.5 mL	kaffir lime rind (see page 229)
½ tsp • 2.5 mL	turmeric
½ tsp • 2.5 mL	freshly ground black pepper

Kebabs

16	jumbo shrimps (11–15 count), shelled and deveined
16	medium presoaked bamboo skewers

1 Combine all marinade ingredients in a non-reactive bowl. Add shrimp and toss gently to coat. Cover and marinate for 1–2 hours at room temperature or up to 4 hours in the refrigerator.

2 Thread each shrimp lengthwise onto a skewer.

3 Grill over medium heat for about 2 minutes per side.

4 Serve with peanut sauce (recipe page 220) or Thai cucumber relish *nam thaeng kwa* (see page 230), sliced onion and lime wedges.

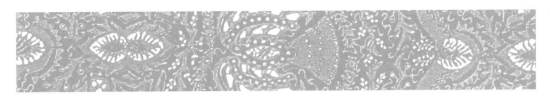

Skewered FISH or SHRIMP balls
Luuk Chin Ping

This popular street food is sold in open air stalls all over Bangkok.
It is usually eaten with a hot dipping sauce called *nam chim pla*.

SERVES 4

1 lb • 500 g	**minced white fish or shrimp meat**
2 Tbsp • 25 mL	**vegetable oil**
1 Tbsp • 15 mL	**cornstarch**
1 Tbsp • 15 mL	**lime juice**
½ tsp • 2.5 mL	**salt**
½ tsp • 2.5 mL	**sugar**
½ tsp • 2.5 mL	**white pepper**
4	**medium presoaked wooden skewers**

1 Mix all food ingredients well until a smooth sticky paste is obtained.

2 Moisten hands with water and roll the paste into small balls about 1 inch (2.5 cm) in diameter. Drop the balls in boiling water and poach for 5 minutes. Drain.

3 Thread 4 balls onto each skewer. Brush with vegetable oil and grill over medium heat, turning frequently until slightly charred, 5–10 minutes.

4 Serve as an appetizer with peanut dipping sauce *nam chim pla* (see page 229) or as a main dish with noodles, vegetables and salad.

• *The name for skewers in Thai is* ping *and the most popular satays sold in the street are referred to as* Nua Ping *(beef),* Kai Ping *(chicken),* Moo Ping *(pork),* Pla Muk Ping *(squid),* Luk Chin Ping *(meat or fish balls),* Gun Kai Ping *(chicken gizzards),* Tub Kai Ping, *(chicken liver) and* Kung Ping *(shrimps).*

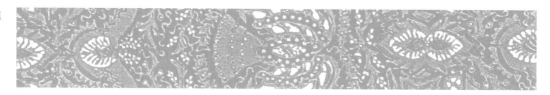

SKEWERED PORK

Nem Nuong

SERVES 4–6

Dipping Sauce

½ cup • 125 mL	soy sauce
⅓ cup • 75 mL	lemon or lime juice
¼ cup • 50 mL	fish sauce
1 tsp • 5 mL	garlic, minced
1 tsp • 5 mL	sugar
1	finely shredded carrot

Kebabs

1 lb • 500 g	minced lean pork
½ cup • 125 mL	finely chopped water chestnuts
2 Tbsp • 25 mL	vegetable oil
2 Tbsp • 25 mL	soy sauce
1 Tbsp • 15 mL	fish sauce
1 Tbsp • 15 mL	finely chopped green onion
1 tsp • 5 mL	salt
1 tsp • 5 mL	sugar
1 tsp • 5 mL	chili oil
1 tsp • 5 mL	ginger paste
1 tsp • 5 mL	garlic paste
1 tsp • 5 mL	ground roasted peanuts

12	long, thick, presoaked bamboo skewers
	lettuce leaves, chopped cilantro, chopped mint and chopped green onion for serving

1 Combine all dipping sauce ingredients in a non-reactive bowl and set aside.

2 Place all kebab ingredients, except for lettuce, cilantro, mint and onions for garnish in a food processor and blend to a smooth but coarse paste. Refrigerate for 2 hours to firm up.

3 Divide the mixture into 12 portions. Moisten hands with water and wrap each portion around the top third of a skewer to form a sausage-like shape.

4 Grill skewers over medium heat for 8–10 minutes, turning frequently to ensure that all sides are uniformly brown and crusted.

5 On a platter, place lettuce leaves, chopped cilantro and mint leaves, and chopped green onion. Slide cooked pork kebabs off each skewer onto a lettuce leaf; wrap each leaf around each kebab along with cilantro, mint and green onion.

6 Serve with a dipping sauce or hot chili sauce.

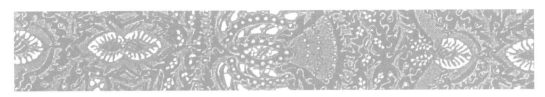

Skewered SHRIMP BALLS

Chao Tom

SERVES 4–8

1 Tbsp • 15 mL	vegetable oil
3	shallots, minced
2 Tbsp • 25 mL	chopped green onion
2 lb • 1 kg	small shrimps, peeled and pat dried
2	egg whites
2 Tbsp • 25 mL	cornstarch or tapioca
1 Tbsp • 15 mL	sugar
2 tsp • 10 mL	fish sauce *nuoc mam* (see page 230)
1 tsp • 5 mL	sesame oil
1 tsp • 5 mL	garlic paste
1 tsp • 5 mL	ginger paste
½ tsp • 2.5 mL	salt
½ tsp • 2.5 mL	white pepper
2 Tbsp • 25 mL	sesame seeds mixed with 2 Tbsp (25 mL) fine breadcrumbs for coating
1 Tbsp • 15 mL	chili oil mixed with an equal amount sesame oil for basting
16	medium presoaked bamboo skewers

1 Heat vegetable oil in a pan over medium-high heat and sauté shallots and green onion for 1 minute.

2 Transfer to a food processor and add shrimps, egg whites, cornstarch, sugar, fish sauce, sesame oil, garlic, ginger, salt and pepper. Blend to a thick paste. Place in the refrigerator for an hour to firm up.

3 Moisten hands with water and make balls 1 inch (2.5 cm) in diameter. Roll them in the sesame seed and breadcrumb mixture. Thread 3–4 balls onto each skewer.

4 Grill over medium-high heat for 5 minutes, turning and basting with a mixture of chili oil and sesame oil frequently. (The skewers can be steamed for 3–5 minutes instead of grilling, if preferred.)

5 Serve as an appetizer with dipping sauce *nuoc mam cham* (see page 230) or as a main course with salad and rice noodles.

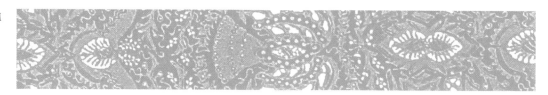

SHRIMP LOLLIPOPS
Chao Tom Lui Mia

SERVES 4–6

1 lb • 500 g	small shrimps, peeled and pounded
½ cup • 125 mL	fish sauce *(nuoc mam)* (see page 230)
1	medium onion, finely chopped
1 tsp • 5 mL	garlic paste
¼ cup • 50 mL	finely chopped cilantro stems
¼ lb • 125 g	pork fat
1	egg white
2 tsp • 10 mL	sugar
¾ tsp • 4 mL	salt
¼ tsp • 1 mL	white pepper
12	sugar cane pieces, 4 inches (10 cm) long
2 Tbsp • 25 mL	chopped green onion for garnish

1 Marinate shrimps in fish sauce for 30 minutes. Drain fish sauce and discard.

2 In a mortar, pound shrimps with onion, garlic, cilantro and pork fat until a thick paste is obtained. Add egg white, sugar, salt and pepper to this paste and mix well. Place in the refrigerator for an hour to firm up.

3 Wet hands and divide mixture into 12 portions. Wrap one portion around each sugar cane piece to form an elongated lollipop.

4 Grill skewers over medium heat for 8–10 minutes, turning frequently to ensure that all sides are golden brown.

5 Serve with chili sauce and cilantro leaves. Sprinkle with chopped green onion.

• *This is a famous Vietnamese delicacy. Minced shrimps are wrapped around a piece of sugar cane, which acts as a skewer for grilling. Sugar cane pieces are available in Chinese or oriental food shops*

• *Other popular Vietnamese satays include* Nem Nuong *(pork),* Bo La Lot *(beef),* Muc Nuong *(squid) and* Tom Nuong Xa *(shrimps).*

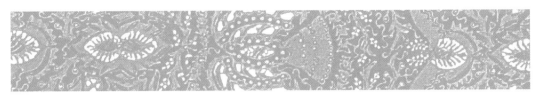

SKEWERED BEEF

Bo Nuong Lui

Marinade

2	stalks lemon grass (white portion only), chopped
1	medium onion or 4 shallots, chopped
4	garlic cloves
2	fresh red chilies, seeded
2 Tbsp • 25 mL	fish sauce *(nuoc mam)* (see page 230)
1 Tbsp • 15 mL	vegetable oil
1 Tbsp • 15 mL	sesame oil
1 Tbsp • 15 mL	sugar
½ tsp • 2.5 mL	freshly ground black pepper

Kebabs

¼ cup • 50 mL	vegetable oil for frying
1 lb • 500 g	beefsteak, cut into strips 4-inches (10-cm) long, ¼-inch (.5-cm) thick and 1-inch (2.5-cm) wide
12	medium presoaked bamboo skewers
	chili-lime dipping sauce *(nouc mam toi ot)* (see page 230)
	lettuce, angel hair noodles, cilantro leaves, mint leaves, sliced cucumber and bean sprouts for serving

1 Combine all marinade ingredients in a blender and process to a smooth paste.

2 Heat vegetable oil in a frying pan on high heat, add marinade paste and fry for about 5 minutes, until it turns slightly brown. Turn off heat and let the pan cool.

3 Weave each beef strip onto a skewer and place in a shallow non-reactive dish. Pour marinade paste, including all the oil, in the frying pan over the skewers. Gently turn skewers a few times to ensure paste coats beef thoroughly. Cover and marinate in the refrigerator overnight.

4 Grill skewers over high heat for 1–2 minutes per side, turning only once. Transfer the cooked beef from skewers to a plate.

5 Make a bed of lettuce, angel hair noodles, cilantro, cucumber, bean sprouts and fresh mint leaves. Place the beef on top and roll into a small wrap. Dip rolls in small bowl of chili-lime sauce and eat by hand.

East Asia

This region includes China (including Taiwan, Macao and Hong Kong), the Korean Peninsula, Japan, Mongolia, far eastern Russia and Siberia. The cuisines of eastern Russia, Siberia and Mongolia are not well known in the West and it is doubtful that kebab cookery has made any inroads in that part of the world. The so-called Mongolian barbecue or grill is not actually Mongolian in origin; it is said to be a Chinese or possibly American invention.

There is no doubt that the impact of Chinese culinary practices on all East Asian and Southeast Asian countries has been huge. But although China, Korea and Japan share common ingredients in their cooking—rice, noodles, soy sauce, tofu or bean curd, ginger, garlic, rice vinegar and sesame oil— the cuisine of each country has its own distinctive characteristics. The highly developed regional characteristics of Chinese cooking, the simplicity and visual elegance of Japanese dishes and the seductive spiciness of Korean food are legendary.

Skewer cooking does not form part of traditional Chinese cuisine, but in big cities like Beijing and Shanghai kebabs are available in small eateries and restaurants run by Uighurs, an ethnic Muslim minority group from Xinjiang province. Xinjiang, once known as East Turkistan, is a vast, partially inhabited region in the northwestern corner of China. The Uighurs form the largest ethnic group in Xinjiang that is ethnically and culturally distinct from Han Chinese. Uighurs are predominantly Muslim, have Turkish roots and speak a language that is derived from Turkish. They have been clamoring for independence from China, or at least for a semi-autonomous status, but have been put down forcefully by the Chinese authorities.

Skewered mutton pieces grilled over an open fire are a traditional food of the Uighur people that is gaining popularity in other parts of China. In Beijing, there is a large population of Uighurs, and several kebab stalls or open-air restaurants in side streets and alleyways sell mutton kebabs and mutton specialties laced with Xinjiang spices. These stalls come to life after six in the evening and provide inexpensive and authentic lamb kebabs threaded onto bamboo skewers and grilled without marinating. They are basted with a chili sauce during grilling and then rolled in a mixture of roasted cumin, anise and sesame seeds. Although pork is the favorite meat in China, Uighur restaurants serve only lamb, beef and chicken because of religious considerations.

Generally the kebab trade operates after sundown and is active until dawn in most places in China. A pork version of kebab called *zhu rou chuan* is sold from street stalls near beaches in Qingdao. Skewered squid called *dianko youyu* or *wuu zei* is another popular street food; it is either grilled over an open fire or on a hot plate, brushed with a hot sauce, sprinkled with a mixture of roasted cumin and anise seeds, then trimmed into small pieces with scissors before it is served to customers.

Being an island nation, Japan has developed a cuisine that focuses on fish, shellfish and other seafood. Meat has not traditionally held a central role, but with the increasing popularity of Western-style fast foods and imports of relatively inexpensive beef and poultry from abroad, chicken and beef have become a part of the Japanese diet.

Kushiyaki, cooking food on skewers (*kushi* is the Japanese word for skewer), has been practiced in Japan for hundreds of years, so it is not surprising that a kebab culture of sorts flourishes in Japan. The Japanese equivalent is *yakitori*, and stalls and bars called *yakitori-ya* serve bite-size pieces of chicken or other meats threaded onto a bamboo skewer and grilled over charcoal. Traditionally, yakitori refers to chicken or chicken parts *(tori)* threaded on skewers and grilled *(yaki)*, and although chicken is the main item in bars and stalls, an array of other meats and vegetables is also offered. The meat is sometimes marinated in a mixture of soy sauce and sake and sometimes not marinated at all but brushed with a dipping sauce and/or dunked into the dipping sauce before serving. Yakitori as street food has developed over hundreds of years, and food vendors called *yatai* pushing carts with portable charcoal braziers are a familiar sight in both large cities and smaller towns in Japan.

Ordinarily yakitori bars serve bamboo skewers threaded with no more than four small pieces of meat that, after grilling, are dipped in either a sweet dipping sauce called *tare* made of mirin, soy sauce, sake and sugar or a salty dipping sauce called *shio*. The secret of a good yakitori is in the taste the dipping sauce imparts to the finished product, and in some yakitori outlets, the leftover dipping sauce is so good that it is used over and over again after boiling, straining and topping up from time to time. Often a spice mixture with red peppers called *shichimi* is sprinkled over the skewered meat in addition to or instead of a dipping sauce. A wide variety of skewered items is available in a well-established *yakitori-ya*; popular ones are *negima* (chicken with onion), *sasami* (chicken breast), *momo* (chicken leg), *nankotsu* (chicken with bone), *sunagimo* (chicken gizzard), *motsu* (chicken giblets), *rebaa* (chicken liver), *kawa* (chicken skin), *aigamo* (duck), *tan* (beef tongue), *kushikatsu* (fried beef), *fire* (beef fillet), *minomiso* (beef tripe), *butabara* (pork tenderloin), *shinzo* (pork heart), *siro* (pork leg) and *aka* (pork liver). Yakitori-ya are a Japanese institution similar to the tapas bars of Spain. They are drinking establishments rather than restaurants, often identifiable by a red lantern hung outside their main entrance. Most yakitori bars do not open until 5 p.m. and are popular gathering places for office workers returning home in the early evening, who treat themselves to skewered delicacies, usually washed down with beer or sake. Most yakitori bars are informal, loud and boisterous places where the atmosphere is anything but sedate. They are fun places for people to go and unwind after a hard day at the office.

Korea, a peninsula sandwiched between China and Japan, is influenced by both countries. Surrounded by some of the most bountiful seas in the world, Koreans have developed a preference for fish, shellfish and other seafood, the mainstays of their diet. Beef is preferred over any other meat and barbecued beef (*pul-goki* or *bulgogi*) is a most popular Korean dish. Food, particularly that of South Korea, is highly seasoned with soy sauce, soybean paste, salt, garlic, ginger, red pepper or chilies and sesame oil.

All sorts of skewered foods, called *o-deng*, are sold by the street vendors known as *pojangmacha* throughout South Korea. Most popular is the Korean version of spicy skewered beef known as *yuk sanjok* (*yuk* refers to beef and *sanjok* means skewer), which is pan-fried but can be grilled over hot coals. Another popular preparation is chicken kebabs, known as *dakkochi* or *dak sanjok*, which are boneless pieces of chicken breast or thigh marinated in red pepper paste, threaded onto bamboo skewers, grilled over a hot plate and served with a sweet spicy sauce. Spicy grilled squid on skewers called *ojingaugui* are also a favorite, particularly in food stalls near the seashore. Skewers of meat and seafood alternating with vegetables like cabbage, hot peppers, bell peppers and mushrooms are also popular street foods and are called *sogogi* or *soegogi sanjok* (beef), *toejigogi sanjok* (pork) and *saeu sanjok* (shrimp).

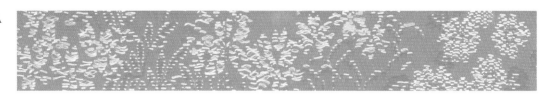

Spicy SKEWERED LAMB

Yang Rou Chuan

SERVES 4

Marinade

¼ cup • 50 mL	chopped cilantro
2 Tbsp • 25 mL	light soy sauce
2 Tbsp • 25 mL	hoisin sauce
1 Tbsp • 15 mL	rice wine or dry sherry
1 tsp • 5 mL	garlic paste
1 tsp • 5 mL	ginger paste
1 tsp • 5 mL	crushed dry red chili
1 tsp • 5 mL	toasted ground Szechwan peppercorn
1 tsp • 5 mL	curry powder
1 tsp • 5 mL	sugar

Kebabs

2 lb • 1 kg	boneless leg of lamb cut into 1½-inch (4-cm) pieces
8	long metal or presoaked bamboo skewers

1 Combine all marinade ingredients in a large non-reactive bowl. Add lamb and toss well to ensure all pieces are thoroughly coated with marinade. Cover and marinate for up to 2 hours at room temperature or overnight in the refrigerator.

2 Drain marinade and reserve. Thread 5–6 pieces of lamb onto each skewer.

3 Grill over medium heat for about 10 minutes or until lamb is well browned on the outside and pink inside, turning and basting with reserved marinade occasionally.

4 Serve with *nang* bread, sprinkle kebabs with Xinjiang seasoning *ziran* (page 231) if available.

• *These kebabs are a speciality of Uighur Muslims and are sold throughout China.*

• *In Chinese* rou *refers to meat and* chuang *or* chuan *means a skewer. Lamb kebabs are called* yang rou chuang, *beef kebabs are referred to as* niu rou chuang *and chicken kebobs are known as* ji rou chuang. *These kebabs are not marinated but are seasoned with salt, chili powder, black pepper and a special herb called* ziran *that imparts a unique anise-like flavor. Ziran is available in some Chinese food stores.*

SKEWERED MEATBALLS

Tsukune

Dipping Sauce

1 cup • 250 mL	**tamari (Japanese soy sauce)**
¼ cup • 50 mL	**sake**
¼ cup • 50 mL	**mirin**
2 Tbsp • 25 mL	**sugar**

Kebabs

1 lb • 500 g	**ground chicken**
3 Tbsp • 45 mL	**soy sauce**
3 Tbsp • 45 mL	**dashi (Japanese soup stock)**
1 Tbsp • 15 mL	**mirin**
2 tsp • 10 mL	**cornstarch**
1 tsp • 5 mL	**grated fresh ginger**
8–12	**small presoaked bamboo skewers**

SERVES 4–6

1 Mix all dipping sauce ingredients in a small saucepan and bring to a boil. Cook until sugar is dissolved. Cool and transfer to a tall narrow container that can accommodate a bamboo skewer with meat.

2 In a bowl, mix chicken, soy sauce, dashi, mirin, cornstarch and ginger. Knead with hands, if necessary, to obtain a uniform mixture. Refrigerate for at least 1 hour to allow flavors to develop.

3 Moisten hands with water and shape meat mixture into small balls about 1 inch (2.5 cm) in diameter. Set aside. Bring water to a boil in a saucepan. Drop in meatballs, a few at a time, and cook until they rise to the surface. Drain and allow to cool.

4 Thread 2–3 balls onto each skewer. Immerse in the dipping sauce and then grill over high heat, turning constantly until meatballs are golden brown on all sides.

5 Immerse skewers once again in dipping sauce and serve. Traditionally tsukune is served with the yolk of a raw egg smeared over the cooked meat.

Skewered GRILLED CHICKEN
Yakitori

SERVES 4–6

Dipping Sauce

½ cup • 125 mL	tamari (Japanese soy sauce)
¼ cup • 50 mL	mirin
1 Tbsp • 15 mL	sugar

Kebabs

1 lb • 500 g	boneless chicken breast or thigh cut into 1-inch (2.5-cm) pieces
½ lb • 250 g	chicken livers cut into 1-inch (2.5-cm) pieces
6	Chinese black mushrooms, soaked and cut into half
4	small green peppers, seeded and cut into 1–1½-inch (2.5–4-cm) squares
2	green onions, white portion only cut into 1½-inch (4-cm) pieces
16	small presoaked bamboo skewers

1 Combine dipping sauce ingredients in a saucepan and bring to boil over medium heat. Cook uncovered until sauce is reduced by two-thirds, Cool and store in a tall jar that can accommodate a filled skewer.

2 Thread 12 skewers with 3–4 pieces of chicken breast, and liver, leaving a little space between pieces for even cooking. Thread remaining 4 skewers with alternating mushroom, green pepper and onion. Thread onion crosswise on the skewer.

3 Grill chicken skewers over medium heat for about 1 minute per side. Remove skewers and dip into jar with sauce. Return skewers to grill and cook for another minute or two per side until the chicken is tender but not burnt. Brush vegetable skewers with sauce and grill until cooked.

4 Arrange skewers on a large platter and serve with *schichimi togarashi*—a mixture of powdered red pepper and six other dry spices (see page 231).

• *A typical yakitori consists of skewered pieces of various parts of chicken such as breast, thigh, skin, liver, gizzard and heart, and a combination of seasonal vegetables.*

Skewered CHICKEN with ONION

Negima Yakitori

Dipping Sauce

½ cup • 125 mL	tamari (Japanese soy sauce)
¼ cup • 50 mL	sake
¼ cup • 50 mL	mirin
¼ cup • 50 mL	chicken stock
4	fresh ginger slices
2 Tbsp • 25 mL	sugar
2 Tbsp • 25 mL	cornstarch

Kebabs

1 lb • 500 g	boneless chicken breast or thigh, cut into pieces, 1–1½ inches (2.5–4 cm)
4	green onions, cut into 1½-inch (4-cm) pieces
8	small or medium presoaked bamboo skewers

1 Combine all dipping sauce ingredients except cornstarch in a saucepan. Bring to a boil over medium heat and cook until the liquid is reduce by half. Dissolve cornstarch in 1 Tbsp (15 mL) cold water, add to reduced liquid and continue cooking until a clear, thick, syrupy liquid is obtained. Discard ginger slices and pour liquid into a tall jar with a wide mouth.

2 Thread 3 pieces of chicken alternating with 2 green onion pieces onto each skewer. Thread onion crosswise onto the skewer. Brush with dipping sauce.

3 Grill over medium heat for about 2 minutes per side or until chicken is cooked.

4 Dip the skewers in dipping sauce. Serve as an appetizer or as part of a main meal with rice.

• *This is by far the most popular type of yakitori and a mainstay at yakitori bars.*

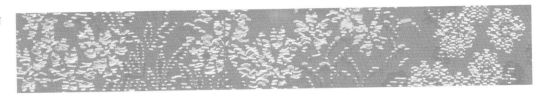

BEEF and ONION SKEWERS

Gyuniku no Kushiyaki

Marinade

¼ cup • 50 mL	tamari (Japanese soy sauce)
2 Tbsp • 25 mL	mirin
2 Tbsp • 25 mL	sake
1 Tbsp • 15 mL	sugar
1 tsp • 5 mL	minced garlic
1 tsp • 5 mL	minced fresh ginger

Kebabs

1 lb • 500 g	beef fillet, flank or top sirloin steak, cut into 1-inch (2.5-cm) cubes
10	green onions (white part only), cut into 1½-inch (4-cm) pieces
10	small presoaked bamboo skewers

1 Combine all marinade ingredients in a non-reactive bowl. Add beef cubes and toss well to coat. Cover and marinate in the refrigerator for at least 6 hours.

2 Remove meat and reserve marinade. Thread 3 pieces of beef alternating with 2 onion pieces onto each skewer (thread onion pieces crosswise on the skewers).

3 Brush skewers with reserved marinade. In a small saucepan boil remaining marinade until it becomes a thick, syrupy sauce.

4 Grill skewers over high heat for 2–3 minutes per side. Brush with marinade sauce before serving.

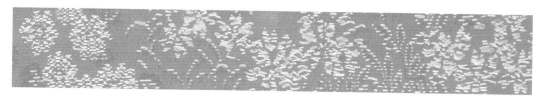

Japanese CHICKEN KEBABS

Tori no Kushiyaki

Marinade

2 Tbsp • 25 mL	tamari (Japanese soy sauce)
2 Tbsp • 25 mL	mirin
2 Tbsp • 25 mL	sake
1 tsp • 5 mL	sugar
1 tsp • 5 mL	minced garlic
1 tsp • 5 mL	minced ginger

Kebabs

1 lb • 500 g	chicken breasts cut into 1¼-inch (3-cm) pieces
1	medium onion, quartered and layers separated
2	red bell peppers cut into 1½-inch (4-cm) squares
8	medium presoaked bamboo skewers

Dipping Sauce

¼ cup • 50 mL	soy sauce
¼ cup • 50 mL	mirin
1 tsp • 5 mL	sugar
1 tsp • 5 mL	grated fresh ginger

1 Combine all marinade ingredients in a non-reactive bowl. Add chicken and toss well to coat. Cover and marinate in the refrigerator for 2–4 hours and preferably overnight.

2 Prepare dipping sauce by combining all ingredients and set aside.

3 Remove chicken and reserve marinade. Thread 3–4 pieces of chicken alternating with onion and red pepper onto each skewer.

4 Grill skewers over medium heat for 6–8 minutes, turning and basting with reserved marinade frequently.

5 Serve with rice, dipping sauce and red pickled ginger.

• *Red pickled ginger is a common Japanese relish eaten with sushi. It is available in Japanese or Asian food stores.*

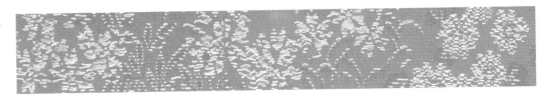

Spicy BEEF SKEWERS

Yuk Sanjok

SERVES 4–6

2 lb • 1 kg	beef tenderloin, flank or top sirloin steak
1 Tbsp • 15 mL	sugar
¼ cup • 50 mL	soy sauce
2 Tbsp • 25 mL	sesame oil
2 tsp • 10 mL	garlic paste
1 tsp • 5 mL	red chili flakes
½ tsp • 2.5 mL	ground black pepper
6	green onions (white and firm green part only), cut into 2-inch (5-cm) pieces
12	medium presoaked bamboo skewer
2 Tbsp • 25 mL	toasted sesame seeds

1 Cut beef into strips across the grain, about ¼–½ inch (1–1.5 cm) thick, 1 inch (2.5 cm) wide and 2 inches (5 cm) long. Sprinkle sugar over beef, mix and let stand at room temperature for 30 minutes.

2 Combine soy sauce, sesame oil, garlic, chili flakes and pepper in a bowl. Add beef and green onion pieces, toss gently to coat and refrigerate for an hour.

3 Thread 2 or more pieces of beef alternating with onion onto each skewer.

4 Grill over high heat for 6–8 minutes, turning and brushing with sesame oil frequently.

5 Roll cooked skewers in toasted sesame seeds and serve with rice, salad and *kimchi* (see page 229).

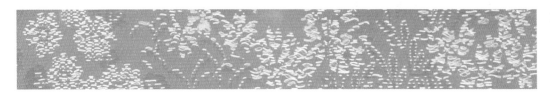

BEEF and VEGETABLE skewers

Soegogi Sanjok

Marinade

½ cup • 125 mL	rice wine
¼ cup • 50 mL	lemon juice
3 Tbsp • 45 mL	soy sauce
2 Tbsp • 25 mL	corn syrup
1 Tbsp • 15 mL	sugar
1 Tbsp • 15 mL	toasted sesame seeds
1 tsp • 5 mL	minced garlic
1 tsp • 5 mL	freshly ground black pepper
1 Tbsp • 15 mL	finely chopped green onion

Kebabs

2 lb • 1 kg	beef tenderloin, cut into strips 2 inches (5 cm) long, 1 inch (2.5 cm) wide and ⅛ inch (0.3 cm) thick
6	green onions (white and firm green part only), cut into 3-inch (7-cm) pieces
1	napa cabbage, cut into chunks 3 inches (7 cm) by 1 inch (2.5 cm)
2	green bell peppers, cut into 2-inches (5-cm) squares
2	hot red peppers, seeded and cut in half
12	medium presoaked bamboo skewers
1 Tbsp • 15 mL	sesame oil

1 Combine all marinade ingredients in a shallow non-reactive dish.

2 Thread 2–3 beef strips alternating with onion, napa cabbage and red and green peppers onto each skewer. Place the skewers in a shallow dish and cover them with the marinade. Marinate at room temperature for at least 30 minutes or longer in the refrigerator.

3 Remove skewers from the marinade. Grill over high heat for 2–3 minutes per side, brushing occasionally with the marinade.

4 Transfer skewers to a serving dish, sprinkle with warmed sesame oil and serve with white rice.

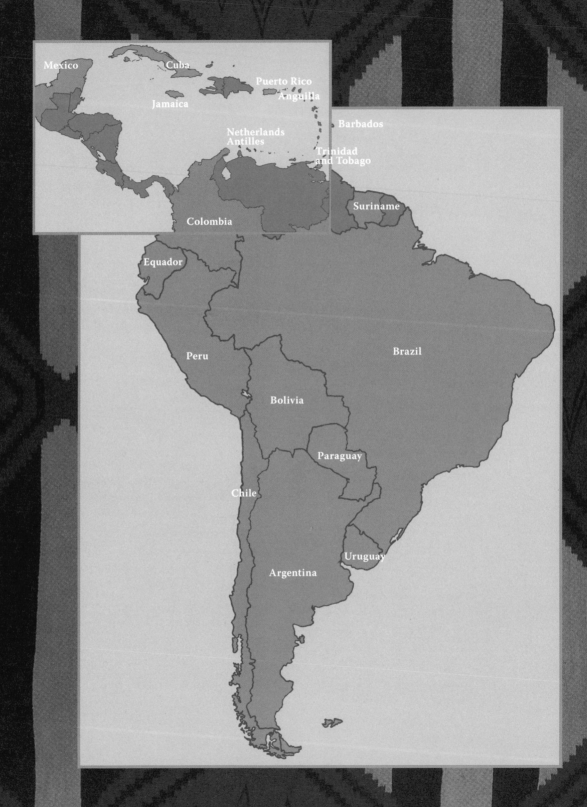

Latin America and the Caribbean

This region includes countries of South America, Central America and Mexico, and the Spanish-, French- and English-speaking islands of the Caribbean. A large portion of Latin America's population is a mixture of native Indians, African slaves, Spanish and Portuguese colonizers and the settlers who came from Europe, the Middle East and Asia. Native Indians constitute a significant portion of the population of Peru, Bolivia, Ecuador and Colombia. Other South American countries have a sizeable mestizo (mixed Amerindian-Spanish) population, and people of African descent live all over the northern part of the South American continent and the Caribbean. Argentina is predominantly European, whereas Brazil is mostly Creole. Inhabitants of Central America and Mexico are represented by remnants of the indigenous Aztec and Mayan people, mestizos, Africans and Europeans.

This extraordinary amalgamation of racial groups and cultures has created a vibrant, varied and rich cuisine throughout the region. Although Latin American cooking varies widely from country to country, there are some similarities. Common ingredients, such as corn, potatoes, beans, tomatoes, squash and chilies, were eaten by the indigenous people. The Spanish influence is seen in spices and herbs like cumin, cinnamon, nutmeg, anise, oregano, saffron, cilantro and parsley, and foods such as dried shrimp, cheese, lamb, beef and salt cod. The cooking of Nicaragua, Guatemala, Panama, Costa Rica and El Salvador is closer to Spanish cooking than that of Mexico, Peru, Colombia, Chile, Argentina, Paraguay and Uruguay. Brazil boasts a different style reflecting Portuguese, African and native Indian influences. Portuguese colonists who imported West African slaves to work on sugar plantations in Brazil also introduced spices, nuts and seeds from Africa. Because of its long Pacific coastline, rich with marine life, seafood is an important component of Chilean cuisine.

Although corn, chilies, beans and tomatoes are basic ingredients, Mexican cooking is diverse, and each region has its own unique ingredients, cooking style, tastes and textures. In the south a variety of dried chilies are incorporated into stews and intricate sauces; in central Mexico *(Altiplano)* there is a blend of Aztec and Spanish cooking; and the Yucatan Peninsula favors sauces based on fruits and chicken and pork cooked in banana leaves. Along the Pacific coast, the emphasis is on fish and seafood dishes. Northern states bordering the United States and referred to as *El Norte* are known for cattle ranching; beef is the foremost meat followed by kid, pork and lamb. Barbecuing and grilling over hardwoods, such as mesquite, that impart a pleasant smoky flavor to meat are the preferred methods of cooking.

The Caribbean is the great arc of islands, each distinctive in its own way, stretching from Florida to the South American mainland. Their cuisines are molded not only by the foods originally available on each island, but also by their colonial past. Since Columbus discovered the Caribbean Islands over 500 years ago, waves of European colonizers have left their mark on each island they occupied.

The Dutch and English colonizers imported large numbers of African slaves to work on plantations and farms on the islands between the 16th and 18th centuries. This migration had a significant impact on the demographic, cultural, social and culinary characteristics of each island. With the abolition of slavery in the mid-19th century, the colonizers turned to importing indentured labor from the East Indies, India and China, further reshaping the Caribbean island's culture. Other immigrants came to the Caribbean to work, visit or eventually settle, adding to the mix.

The cuisines of Cuba, Puerto Rico and the Dominican Republic are strongly influenced by Spanish traditions. In Cuba food tends to be light and flavorful; a fried mixture of tomatoes, green pepper, onion, salt, garlic, bay leaf, cumin, oregano and olive oil, known as *sofrito*, is the base of most Cuban dishes. The French Caribbean islands of Martinique, Guadeloupe, Haiti and Saint Martin have an intriguing blend of Creole and French cooking. The Dutch Antilles, which includes the islands of Aruba, Bonaire, Curacao, St. Maarten, St. Eustatius and Saba, have a mélange of African, Portuguese, Venezuelan, East Indian, Chinese and Indonesian cuisines. British Caribbean cuisine, particularly that of Trinidad and Tobago, Jamaica and Barbados, is a fusion of many ethnic traditions, including Arawak Indian, Spanish, East Indian, Chinese, Middle Eastern and British.

With few exceptions, kebab cookery has not made significant inroads in Latin America and the Caribbean. Despite the fact that grilling meat is a way of life in much of South America, particularly in Argentina, Uruguay, Brazil and Paraguay, little attention has been paid to cooking small pieces of marinated meat on skewers. Instead, large chunks of beef, lamb and pork with little seasoning are grilled on vertical spikes in front of a campfire *(asado)* or over wood-burning grills *(parrilla)*. The classic Argentine-style barbecue *(asado)*, involves traditional beef and meats such as lamb, chicken, kidneys, sweetbread and sausages cooked slowly over low heat. The meat is seldom marinated and no barbecue sauce is used; it is seasoned only with salt and black pepper before grilling and served with a spicy sauce called *chimichurri* (recipe page 223). Traditional barbecue in Uruguay, Paraguay and Brazil is similar. In Brazil barbecue *(churrasco)* involves grilling large chunks of beef and pork on spits and serving these with spicy Brazilian sausages. Brazilians do not generally use sauces or marinades, but rub or sprinkle sea salt over red meat before or during grilling. Some restaurants *(churrascarias)* specializing in Brazilian barbecue now include beef, lamb, chicken and even seafood kebabs in their menu.

In Mexico's El Norte region, beef kebabs known as *alhambres* are popular due to an abundance of beef and its residents' love of grilling and barbecuing. In Peru, kebabs are a favorite street food, particularly the famous *anticuchos*, which are regarded as Peru's national snack. *Anticuchos* traditionally consist of skewered grilled llama hearts, but more often they include pieces of beef heart or other tender cuts of beef marinated in a spicy marinade. *Anticuchos* are the Peruviuan equivalent of hot dogs in America. Throngs at the bull ring at Plaza de Toros or the football stadium in Lima buy them from stalls or carts and wash them down with cold beer or a traditional Peruvian drink *pisco sour*.

In the Caribbean beef is neither cheap nor easily available. Instead, pork, goat, chicken, fish and shellfish are consumed. On the island of Puerto Rico, most food is imported from the United States, and to some extent an Americanized diet has replaced more traditional foods, particularly among young people. Traditional cookery *(cocina criolla)* is mild and based on herbs and spices like cilantro, oregano, lime, ginger, garlic, cumin, cloves and cinnamon. Kebabs known as *pinchos*, the fast food of Puerto Rico, are mostly made of pork or chicken cubes marinated in a multipurpose sauce called *adobo*, grilled and served on a slice of long bread called *pan criollo*, similar to a French baguette. They are a popular treat at the Hiram Bithorn baseball stadium in San Juan, where they compete successfully with hot dogs and other American fast foods. Pinchos of beef and seafoods are also sold in roadside stalls and at the beach-front restaurants in Puerto Rico.

In Barbados and Trinidad and Tobago, you can purchase mangrove oyster kebabs and carnival kebabs, whereas in the islands of the Dutch Antilles kebabs with strange names like *lambchi* and *boonchi* and *boka dushi* can be found. In Jamaica, which is known for its jerk spices, jerk huts or shacks line the roadside throughout the island and serve baked or grilled pork, chicken and fish smeared with jerk spices or paste, served with or without skewers.

CARIBBEAN KEBABS

SERVES 4

Marinade

½ cup • 125 mL	mango pulp
3 Tbsp • 45 mL	lime or lemon juice
2 Tbsp • 25 mL	finely minced shallots
2 Tbsp • 25 mL	brown sugar
2 Tbsp • 25 mL	olive oil
1 Tbsp • 15 mL	curry powder
1 Tbsp • 15 mL	garlic paste
½ tsp • 2.5 mL	cayenne pepper
½ tsp • 2.5 mL	salt

Kebabs

2 lb • 1 kg	boneless chicken breasts cut into 1½-inch (4-cm) cubes
1	fresh pineapple cut into 1½-inch (4-cm) pieces
4	firm ripe bananas cut into 1½-inch (4-cm) pieces
1	firm ripe paw paw cut into 1½-inch (4-cm) pieces
8	long metal or presoaked bamboo skewers

1 Combine all marinade ingredients in a non-reactive bowl. Add chicken, toss well, cover and marinate overnight in the refrigerator.

2 Drain marinade and reserve. Thread 4–5 chicken pieces alternating with pineapple, banana and paw paw onto each skewer.

3 Grill over medium heat for 5–7 minutes, turning and brushing with reserved marinade occasionally.

4 Serve with rice or salad.

BEEF KEBABS

Churrasquinhos

Marinade

¼ cup • 50 mL	olive oil
¼ cup • 50 mL	lemon juice
1	medium onion, grated
1 tsp • 5 mL	minced garlic
1 tsp • 5 mL	salt
½ tsp • 2.5 mL	freshly ground black pepper

Kebabs

2 lb • 1 kg	beef tenderloin, cut into 1¼-inch (3-cm) cubes
6	bacon strips, cut into 1-inch (2.5-cm) pieces
8	medium metal skewers
½ cup • 125 mL	farofa (seasoned manioc flour)

1 Mix all marinade ingredients in a large non-reactive bowl. Add beef and toss well to coat. Cover and marinate in the refrigerator for 2–4 hours.

2 Thread about 6 pieces of beef alternating with bacon onto each skewer.

3 Grill over high heat for 3–4 minutes per side, or until slightly brown on the outside.

4 Roll cooked skewers in farofa before serving.

• *Brazilians enjoy the natural flavor of beef. Their beef kebabs are lightly seasoned or marinated for a short time with a mixture of olive oil, lemon juice, salt and pepper, whereas poultry and lamb kebabs are marinated in spicy and rich marinades for as long as 48 hours.*

• *Farofa is manioc meal or flour that is first toasted and then seasoned. It is popular in Brazil, but is also used in other South American countries, particularly with grilled or barbecued meat. Farofa is available in stores that sell Latin American foods.*

BEEF KEBABS

SERVES 6

Marinade

½ cup • 125 mL	pineapple juice
¼ cup • 50 mL	olive oil
2 Tbsp • 25 mL	lemon or lime juice
2 Tbsp • 25 mL	vinegar
2 Tbsp • 25 mL	dark molasses
2 Tbsp • 25 mL	dark rum
1 tsp • 5 mL	salt
½ tsp • 2.5 mL	freshly ground black pepper

Kebabs

2 lb • 1 kg	top sirloin steak cut into 1¼-inch (3-cm) cubes
1	fresh pineapple cut into 1-inch (2.5-cm) cubes
2	green or red bell peppers, seeded and cut into 1½-inch (4-cm) squares
1	medium red onion, quartered and layers separated
2	medium tomatoes, cut into 6 wedges each
12	long metal skewers

1 Combine all marinade ingredients in a non-reactive bowl. Add beef cubes and toss well to coat. Marinate overnight in the refrigerator.

2 Drain marinade and reserve. Thread 4–5 pieces of meat onto each of 6 skewers. Thread pineapple and vegetables separately onto remaining 6 skewers.

3 Grill beef skewers over high heat for 4–5 minutes per side, turning and basting with reserved marinade frequently. Vegetable skewers need less time to cook and should be removed from the grill when slightly charred.

4 Serve over rice pilaf.

CAJUN SHRIMP WITH MANGO   page 196

LAMB ON ROSEMARY SKEWERS   page 197

HALIBUT AND SALMON KEBABS   page 199

THANKSGIVING TURKEY KEBABS   page 201

SHRIMP KEBABS
Pinchos de Camarones

Marinade

½ cup • 125 mL	chopped cilantro
2 Tbsp • 25 mL	guava paste
2 Tbsp • 25 mL	olive oil
2 Tbsp • 25 mL	lime juice
1 Tbsp • 15 mL	chipotle pepper, minced
1	shallot, chopped
1 tsp • 5 mL	garlic paste

Kebabs

2 lb • 1 kg	large shrimps (21–30 count), shelled and deveined
1	fresh pineapple cut into 1-inch (2.5-cm) cubes
12	medium metal or presoaked bamboo skewers
	melted butter for basting

1   Combine all marinade ingredients in a non-reactive bowl. Add shrimps and toss well to coat. Marinate for no more than 1 hour in the refrigerator.

2   Thread 3–4 shrimps alternating with pineapple cubes onto each skewer.

3   Grill over medium heat for about 2 minutes per side. Baste with melted butter and serve with lemon or lime wedges.

• *Either puréed seeded fresh guava or canned guava paste can be used in this recipe. Guava paste is available in stores that sell Caribbean or South American foods.*

PORK KEBABS
Masitas de Puerco

SERVES 6

Marinade

½ cup • 125 mL	lime juice
¼ cup • 50 mL	olive oil
¼ cup • 50 mL	orange juice
¼ cup • 50 mL	chopped fresh flat-leaf parsley
¼ cup • 50 mL	chopped cilantro
1 tsp • 5 mL	garlic paste
1 tsp • 5 mL	ground cumin
1 tsp • 5 mL	red pepper flakes
1 tsp • 5 mL	salt
½ tsp • 2.5 mL	freshly ground black pepper

Kebabs

2 lb • 1 kg	boneless pork loin cut into 1-inch (2.5-cm) cubes
12	medium metal skewers

1 Combine all marinade ingredients in a non-reactive bowl. Add pork cubes and toss well to coat. Cover and marinate in the refrigerator for at least 4 hours or preferably overnight.

2 Drain marinade and reserve. Thread 5–6 pieces of pork on each skewer. Brush with reserved marinade.

3 Grill over medium-high heat for about 8–10 minutes, or until outside of kebabs is brown and inside no longer pink, turning and basting frequently with marinade.

4 Serve with raw sliced onion, lemon or lime wedges sprinkled with chopped cilantro.

• *Traditionally masitas de puerco use shallow-fried or deep-fried pork, instead of grilled.*

LAMB KEBABS
Lambchi and Boonchi

Marinade

½ cup • 125 mL	lime juice
¼ cup • 50 mL	peanut or olive oil
1	medium onion, grated
2	green hot chilies, seeded
1 Tbsp • 15 mL	curry powder
2 tsp • 10 mL	ginger paste
1 tsp • 5 mL	ground cumin
1 tsp • 5 mL	garlic paste
1 tsp • 5 mL	salt
½ tsp • 2.5 mL	freshly ground black pepper

Kebabs

2 lb • 1 kg	boneless leg of lamb cut into 1½-inch (4-cm) pieces
2	green bell peppers cut into 1-inch (2.5-cm) squares
2	red bell peppers, cut into 1-inch (2.5-cm) square
4	bacon strips cut into 1-inch (2.5-cm) pieces
1	fresh pineapple cut into 1-inch (2.5-cm) cubes
8	long metal skewers

1 Blend all marinade ingredients in a blender or food processor and transfer the mixture to a non-reactive bowl. Add lamb pieces and toss well to coat. Cover and refrigerate overnight.

2 Drain marinade and reserve. Thread 5–6 pieces of lamb alternating with green and red peppers, bacon and pineapple onto each skewer.

3 Grill over medium-high heat for 10–12 minutes, turning and basting with reserved marinade occasionally.

4 Serve with rice or roti (see page 230).

• Lambchi *means lamb and* Boonchi *refers to the yard-long bean that is traditionally wrapped around the skewer. This recipe originates from the Dutch Caribbean islands of Aruba, Curacao and Bonaire. It excludes the yard-long bean because it is not generally available.*

JERK PORK and pineapple kebabs

SERVES 4–8

Marinade

½ cup • 125 mL	lime juice
¼ cup • 50 mL	peanut or olive oil
1	medium onion, grated
2	green hot chilies, seeded
1 Tbsp • 15 mL	curry powder
2 tsp • 10 mL	ginger paste
1 tsp • 5 mL	ground cumin
1 tsp • 5 mL	garlic paste
1 tsp • 5 mL	salt
½ tsp • 2.5 mL	freshly ground black pepper
½ tsp • 2.5 mL	ground cinnamon
½ tsp • 2.5 mL	ground nutmeg

Kebabs

2 lb • 1 kg	pork loin cut into 1½-inch (4-cm) cubes
1	fresh pineapple, cut into 1-inch (2.5-cm) pieces
8	long metal skewers
¼ cup • 50 mL	vegetable oil mixed with an equal amount of orange juice for basting

1 Combine all marinade ingredients and purée in a blender to obtain a smooth paste. Add pork and stir well to coat each cube. Cover and refrigerate for at least 4 hours or preferably overnight.

2 Thread 5–6 pieces of meat alternating with pineapple chunks onto each skewer. Grill over medium-high heat for about 10 minutes, turning frequently and basting with oil and orange juice mixture.

3 Serve over rice or with salad.

• *I was served these delicious jerk pork kebabs on bamboo skewers at a roadside eatery just outside the town of Falmouth in Jamaica.*

BEEF SHISH KEBABS

Alhambres de Carne de Res

Marinade

¼ cup • 50 mL	vegetable or olive oil
¼ cup • 50 mL	dry vermouth
2 Tbsp • 25 mL	lemon juice
1 Tbsp • 15 mL	minced garlic
2 tsp • 10 mL	cayenne pepper
1 tsp • 5 mL	salt
½ tsp • 2.5 mL	freshly ground black pepper

Kebabs

2 lb • 1 kg	beef sirloin steak cut into 1½-inch (4-cm) pieces
2	green peppers seeded and cut into 1-inch (2.5-cm) pieces
2	medium onions cut into 1½-inch (4-cm) wedges
8	long metal skewers

1 Combine all marinade ingredients in a non-reactive bowl. Add beef and toss well. Cover and marinate overnight in the refrigerator.

2 Remove beef and reserve marinade. Thread beef pieces alternating with green pepper and onion wedges onto the skewers.

3 Grill over high heat for 5–6 minutes per side, frequently turning and basting with reserved marinade.

4 Serve with salad or rice.

Grilled SKEWERED CHICKEN

Alhambres de Pollo

Marinade

¼ cup • 50 mL	olive or vegetable oil
2 Tbsp • 25 mL	lime juice
2	poblano chilies, seeded and finely minced
1 tsp • 5 mL	garlic paste
1 tsp • 5 mL	salt
½ tsp • 2.5 mL	freshly ground black pepper

Kebabs

2 lb • 1 kg	boneless chicken breasts or thighs cut into 1½-inch (4-cm) cubes
1	green bell pepper, seeded and cut into 1-inch (2.5-cm) squares
1	red bell pepper, seeded and cut into 1-inch (2.5-cm) squares
6	bacon slices cut into 1-inch (2.5-cm) pieces
2	medium onions cut into 1½-inch (4-cm) wedges
8	long metal or presoaked wooden skewers
	extra vegetable oil for basting

1 Combine all marinade ingredients in a non-reactive bowl. Add chicken pieces and toss well to coat. Cover and marinate overnight in the refrigerator.

2 Remove chicken from marinade. Thread chicken pieces alternating with red pepper, green pepper and onion wedges onto the skewers.

3 Grill skewers on medium high heat for 3–4 minutes per side, turning and basting with vegetable oil frequently.

4 Serve with salad or rice.

SHRIMP KEBABS
Brochetas de Camarones

Marinade

¼ cup • 50 mL	olive oil
¼ cup • 50 mL	finely chopped cilantro leaves
¼ cup • 50 mL	Tequila
2 Tbsp • 25 mL	lemon or lime juice
1 Tbsp • 15 mL	minced garlic
1 tsp • 5 mL	salt
½ tsp • 2.5 mL	cayenne pepper

Kebabs

2 lb • 1 kg	large shrimps (21–30 count), peeled and deveined
12	medium metal or presoaked wooden skewers

1 Combine all marinade ingredients in a non-reactive bowl. Add shrimps and toss to coat. Cover and marinate for 1 hour in the refrigerator.

2 Drain marinade and reserve. Thread 4–5 shrimps onto each skewer.

3 Grill over medium heat, basting frequently with reserved marinade. Cook for 2 minutes per side, turning only once.

4 Serve as an appetizer or as a main course with salad or rice.

LAMB KEBABS

Brochetas de Cordero

SERVES 4–8

Marinade

¼ cup • 50 mL	**olive oil**
¼ cup • 50 mL	**chopped cilantro**
2 Tbsp • 25 mL	**balsamic vinegar**
2 tsp • 10 mL	**garlic paste**
2 tsp • 10 mL	**ground cumin**
1 tsp • 5 mL	**dried mint**
1 tsp • 5 mL	**cayenne pepper**
1 tsp • 5 mL	**salt**
½ tsp • 2.5 mL	**freshly ground black pepper**

Kebabs

2 lb • 1 kg	**boneless leg of lamb, excess fat removed and cut into 1½-inch (4-cm) cubes**
2	**red bell peppers, seeded and cut into 1½-inch (4-cm) squares**
8	**jalapeño peppers, seeded and cut in half lengthwise**
8	**long metal skewers**

1 Combine all marinade ingredients in a non-reactive bowl. Add lamb and toss well to coat. Cover and marinate in the refrigerator overnight.

2 Remove lamb and reserve marinade. Thread lamb, red pepper and jalapeño pepper alternately on the skewers. Brush with marinade.

3 Grill over medium-high heat for about 10 minutes, turning and basting with reserved marinade frequently.

4 Serve over rice or salad.

SKEWERED BEEF HEARTS

Anticuchos

Anticuchos are a popular street food in Peru and Bolivia. Although beef or llama hearts are favorite ingredients, other tender cuts of beef, chicken and seafood are also sold.

Marinade

SERVES 4–6

¾ cup • 175 mL	**red wine vinegar**
⅓ cup • 75 mL	**dried red chilies (hontaka or mirasol)**
1	**dried ancho chili**
1	**whole head of garlic, cloves separated**
2 tsp • 10 mL	**ground cumin**
1½ tsp • 7.5 mL	**salt**
⅓ cup • 75 mL	**annatto (achiote) oil**

Kebabs

1	**beef heart, cleaned of fat and gristle, cut into 1-inch (2.5-cm) pieces**
3	**strips bacon**
20	**small metal or presoaked bamboo skewers**

1 Combine vinegar with chilies and let them soak for 30 minutes. Blend peppers, vinegar, garlic, cumin and salt in a blender and process on high speed to obtain a paste. Add annatto oil to the paste and mix well.

2 Place paste in a non-reactive bowl and add beef pieces. Toss to coat each piece, cover and marinate for up to 24 hours in the refrigerator.

3 Remove beef pieces and reserve marinade. In a small pan, boil marinade with bacon strips until most of the liquid has evaporated and only oil and fat from bacon remains. Remove bacon and reserve oil.

4 Thread about 3–4 cubes of beef pieces onto each skewer. Grill over high heat for about 2 minutes per side, brushing with reserved oil on each turn.

5 Serve as an appetizer or as a meal with boiled corn, sweet potato and cassava.

PORK KEBABS
Pinchos de Puerco

SERVES 3

Marinade

¼ cup • 50 mL	**olive oil**
1 Tbsp • 15 mL	**lemon juice**
2 Tbsp • 25 mL	**chopped fresh parsley or cilantro**
½ tsp • 2.5 mL	**paprika**
½ tsp • 2.5 mL	**ground cumin**
½ tsp • 2.5 mL	**dried thyme**
½ tsp • 2.5 mL	**chili powder**
½ tsp • 2.5 mL	**salt**
¼ tsp • 1 mL	**turmeric**
¼ tsp • 1 mL	**freshly ground black pepper**

Kebabs

1 lb • 500 g	**boneless pork loin cut into 1-inch (2.5-cm) cubes**
6	**medium metal skewers**

1 Combine all marinade ingredients in a non-reactive bowl. Add meat pieces and toss well to coat. Marinate in the refrigerator for 4–24 hours, stirring occasionally.

2 Drain marinade and reserve. Thread 4–5 pieces of meat onto each skewer, leaving about ¼ inch (0.5 cm) space between them.

3 Grill over medium-high heat for 10–12 minutes, turning and basting with reserved marinade occasionally, or until meat is cooked and no longer pink inside.

4 Brush each skewer with barbecue sauce of your choice and serve hot on a slice of *pan criollo* (see page 230) or French bread.

PORK KEBABS

Marinade

½ cup • 125 mL	**shelled peanuts or ¼ cup (50 mL) smooth peanut butter**
1	**medium onion, chopped**
3 Tbsp • 45 mL	**olive oil**
3 Tbsp • 45 mL	**soy sauce**
3 Tbsp • 45 mL	**lime juice**
2 Tbsp • 25 mL	**chopped cilantro**
1 Tbsp • 15 mL	**brown sugar**
1 Tbsp • 15 mL	**light or dark rum**
½ tsp • 2.5 mL	**cayenne pepper**
1–2	**green chilies, seeded**

Kebabs

2 lb • 1 kg	**lean boneless pork, cut into 1-inch (2.5-cm) cubes**
12	**medium metal or presoaked bamboo skewers**

1 Blend all marinade ingredients in a food processor, then transfer to a non-reactive bowl. Add pork and toss well to coat each piece thoroughly. Cover and marinate in the refrigerator overnight.

2 Remove meat and reserve marinade. Thread 5–6 pieces onto each skewer. Grill over medium-high heat for about 10 minutes, turning and basting with marinade occasionally or until meat is no longer pink inside.

3 Serve over rice pilaf.

CARNIVAL KEBABS

SERVES 6 *Marinade*

¼ cup • 50 mL	vegetable oil
2 Tbsp • 25 mL	dark rum
2 Tbsp • 25 mL	chopped green onion (white part only)
1 Tbsp • 15 mL	chopped fresh parsley
1 tsp • 5 mL	chopped fresh chives
½ tsp • 2.5 mL	dried thyme
½ tsp • 2.5 mL	salt
½ tsp • 2.5 mL	freshly ground black pepper

Kebabs

2 lb • 1 kg	beef steak (top sirloin or rump) cut into 1-inch (2.5-cm) cubes
1	fresh pineapple cut into 1-inch (2.5 cm) cubes
24	small white onions, boiled for 2 minutes
1	green bell peppers, seeded and cut into 1-inch (2.5-cm) squares
1	red bell peppers, seeded and cut into 1-inch (2.5-cm) squares
12	medium metal or presoaked bamboo skewers
2 Tbsp • 25 mL	melted butter for basting

1 Combine all marinade ingredients in a bowl. Add beef and toss to coat. Cover and marinate for at least 4 hours and preferably overnight in the refrigerator.

2 Remove beef and reserve marinade. Thread meat, alternating with pineapple, onion and both peppers, onto entire length of each skewer.

3 Grill over high heat for about 3–4 minutes per side, turning and basting with reserved marinade frequently. When cooked, brush with melted butter.

4 Serve with rice, potato or salad and a steak sauce of your choice.

Mangrove OYSTER KEBABS

2 Tbsp • 25 mL	**lime juice**
½ tsp • 2.5 mL	**Trinidad hot pepper sauce**
1 tsp • 5 mL	**chopped chives**
24	**shucked mangrove oysters**
12	**bacon strips, cut in half**
8	**small presoaked bamboo skewers**

1 Combine lime juice, pepper sauce and chives in a non-reactive bowl. Brush each oyster with this mixture.

2 Wrap each oyster with a half strip of bacon. Thread 3 wrapped oysters onto each skewer.

3 Grill skewers over medium heat, turning frequently to ensure bacon gets crisp.

4 Brush each skewer again with pepper sauce mixture before serving as an appetizer.

• *Mangrove, or tree, oysters live on the roots of mangrove trees in the intertidal zone. They are considered a delicacy in Trinidad and sold in roadside stalls as kebabs or as oyster cocktails.*

• *Once abundant in mangrove-rich coastal lagoons of Trinidad and Tobago, mangrove oyster stocks have dwindled considerably due to overfishing, mangrove logging and land reclamation. Other oyster species can be substituted in this recipe. Hot pepper sauce is available in food stores specializing in Caribbean foods.*

North America

Only Canada and the United States are included in this section. Although Mexico and the countries of Central America form part of the North American continent, their linguistic, cultural and culinary ties are more with Latin America than with the United States or Canada. Canada and the United States are predominantly English-speaking countries and share many cultural, social, economic and lifestyle characteristics. Both countries are populated by immigrants from all parts of the world who have brought their own diverse cuisines to North America.

Early settlers were mainly from Britain and France. During those first harsh winters, they learned from Native Indians about corn, squashes, pumpkins, beans and other indigenous foods and techniques to preserve them. Combining Old World recipes with new ingredients and cooking styles laid the foundation for the culinary culture of North America.

Subsequent waves of migrants came from other parts of Europe—Italy, Germany, the Netherlands, Poland, Scandinavia, Russia, Armenia, Ukraine, Greece and many other countries. The Atlantic seaboard was the first to be colonized and a west-ward migration then settled the Midwest and the Pacific coast. Many Cubans, Puerto Ricans and other Hispanics from Mexico and South America chose to settle in New York, Florida, Texas and California. The contribution of African and West Indian slaves and immigrants, particularly in the southern United States, has been significant. They brought cooking traditions and ingredients from Africa and the Caribbean and merged them with French and Spanish cuisines to create Creole cooking. Asian migration in the 20th century brought immigrants from China, Japan, Korea, Vietnam, Cambodia, Thailand, the Philippines and the Indian sub-continent.

These immigrants not only added to the cultural diversity and mosaic of nationalities, they also influenced the North American cuisine by introducing new and unfamiliar foods and new cooking techniques in their adopted land. The immigrants settled in various pockets in Canada and the United States, resulting in diverse regional cuisines. This regionalization is more pronounced in the United States because of its climatic variations, geographical terrain and large population base, but by and large there is little difference between what Canadians and Americans eat every day. It may be a fruitless exercise to look for strictly Canadian food because in the Canadian culinary landscape there are few dishes that are identifiable as truly Canadian.

Of all the ethnic foods introduced by immigrants to North America, southern Italian cuisine had perhaps the most profound impact—pizza and spaghetti have become identified as almost American foods. The acceptance of ethnic foods, availability of ingredients from all parts of the world in supermarkets and specialty food stores and the proliferation of ethnic restaurants (particularly Chinese, Italian and Mexican) are testimony that North American cuisine is innovative and evolving.

Cooking food over an open fire—barbecuing—continues to grow in popularity throughout North America. For centuries Native Indians fastened salmon and other fish to planks and barbecued them on an open fire. Now barbecuing is a way of life during the summer months when long daylight hours entice men to display their culinary talent outside. Barbecue grills of all sizes and shapes are patio, deck and backyard fixtures in a majority of North American homes.

In the United States, the art of barbecuing has assumed an importance something akin to religion, particularly in the Midwest, the southern states and Texas. The barbecuing tradition in the Carolinas, Georgia and Alabama owes its origin to African slaves who manned massive barbecue pits and introduced many African and Caribbean spices and seasonings so characteristic of southern cooking. Beef and pork are the main meats for barbecuing in North America, followed by poultry. Lamb and veal are less widely accepted. However, with increasing imports of good-quality lamb from Australia and New Zealand, lamb is gradually gaining popularity among barbecue enthusiasts.

To many people, barbecuing and grilling are synonymous and are often used interchangeably. However, technically speaking, barbecuing involves cooking food slowly at low to medium temperature, rarely exceeding 300°F (150°C), over indirect heat for a long time. Grilling is almost always done over direct heat, usually at high temperatures and for a shorter time.

Kebab cookery, which requires grilling on direct heat, has a foothold in certain ethnic groups, but is not a large part of North American cuisine. Southern Italian immigrants who began arriving in the mid-19th century and settled mostly in upper New York State introduced *spiedies*, a word derived from the Italian word *spiedini* meaning kebabs. Lamb was the original meat but later chicken, beef and pork replaced lamb because people were not as familiar with lamb meat and it was in short supply. Other small ethnic eateries and restaurants sprang up throughout the United States and Canada run by Turks, Greeks, Lebanese and others of Middle Eastern and Asian origin, selling different types of kebabs. However, despite these positive beginnings, kebabs failed to secure a firm foothold in North America.

One possible explanation might be that Americans and Canadians tend to eat large quantities of meat. The abundance and availability of beef, pork and poultry at a reasonable price favors throwing a thick slab of meat on the grill instead of tinkering with small pieces of meat threaded onto a skewer. However, the growing trend to eating healthy foods and cutting down on red meats makes kebab cookery look increasingly attractive. Kebab recipes continue to be included in numerous recent cookbooks and magazines published in North America, but with few regional exceptions, not many kebab recipes can be regarded as truly American or Canadian.

BEEF or PORK SPIEDIES

SERVES 6

Marinade

½ cup • 125 mL	olive oil
¼ cup • 50 mL	red wine vinegar
1	medium onion, coarsely chopped
1 Tbsp • 15 mL	chopped fresh parsley
2 tsp • 10 mL	dried oregano
1 tsp • 5 mL	garlic paste
1 tsp • 5 mL	paprika
1 tsp • 5 mL	freshly ground black pepper
1 tsp • 5 mL	salt
1 tsp • 5 mL	chopped fresh rosemary

Kebabs

2 lb • 1 kg	boneless lean beef or pork cut into 1-inch (2.5-cm) cubes
12	medium metal skewers

1 In a food processor, blend all marinade ingredients. Transfer to a non-reactive bowl. Add meat pieces and toss well to coat. Cover and marinate in the refrigerator for up to 24 hours.

2 Remove meat pieces and thread 5–6 pieces onto each skewer.

3 Grill over medium-high heat for about 4–5 minutes per side, turning frequently.

4 Serve over rice or with salad.

• *This recipe is from Upper New York State where early immigrants from Italy first settled. They introduced lamb kebabs and called them "spiedies," derived from the Italian word,* spiedini, *for kebabs.*

Oriental SEAFOOD KEBABS

Marinade

½ cup • 125 mL	sake
1 Tbsp • 15 mL	sesame oil
1 Tbsp • 15 mL	lemon or lime juice
1 Tbsp • 15 mL	finely chopped cilantro
1 tsp • 5 mL	garlic paste
1 tsp • 5 mL	ginger paste
½ tsp • 2.5 mL	salt

Kebabs

1 lb • 500 g	large shrimps (21–30 count), peeled and deveined
1 lb • 500 g	medium sea scallops
1	large green bell pepper, seeded and cut into 1-inch (2.5-cm) squares
1	large red onion cut into 1½-inch (4-cm) wedges
8	long metal or presoaked wooden skewers
8	cherry tomatoes (optional)

SERVES 4–8

1 Combine all marinade ingredients in a non-reactive bowl. Add shrimps and scallops, toss well and let stand at room temperature for 30 minutes.

2 Drain and save marinade. Thread 3 shrimps and 3 scallops alternating with green pepper and onion onto each skewer. Top with a cherry tomato, if desired.

3 Grill skewers over medium heat, turning and basting with reserved marinade for about 3–4 minutes per side or until shrimps and scallops are cooked.

4 Serve either as appetizers or a main course with rice or salad.

CAJUN SHRIMP with mango

SERVES 4

16	**extra large shrimp (16–20 count), peeled except for tail**
	vegetable oil spray
1	**large ripe mango, cut into ¾-inch (2-cm) cubes**
2 Tbsp • 25 mL	**Cajun spice mix (recipe page 227)**
4	**long metal or presoaked bamboo skewers**

1   Spread all the shrimps in a dish and spray lightly with vegetable oil on both sides.

2   Sprinkle shrimps generously or roll them in the Cajun spice mixture to ensure that both sides are fully coated.

3   Thread 4 shrimps alternating with mango cubes onto each skewer or thread mango cubes inside the curve of each shrimp.

4   Grill over medium heat for about 2–3 minutes per side or until cooked, turning once.

5   Serve as appetizer over fresh spinach leaves or lettuce, garnished with lemon wedges.

• *A very simple recipe tempering the heat of Cajun spice with the sweetness of ripe mango.*

ℒ𝒜ℳ𝔅 on rosemary skewers

Marinade

½ cup • 125 mL	dry red wine
¼ cup • 50 mL	lemon juice
¼ cup • 50 mL	olive oil
1 Tbsp • 15 mL	chopped fresh rosemary
1 Tbsp • 15 mL	finely minced garlic
1 tsp • 5 mL	dried thyme
1 tsp • 5 mL	salt
½ tsp • 2.5 mL	freshly ground black pepper

Kebabs

2 lb • 1 kg	boneless leg of lamb, cut into 1¼-inch (3-cm) pieces
12	rosemary stems 8–10 inches (20–25 cm) long, stripped of all leaves except top 1 inch (2.5 cm)

SERVES 6

1 Combine all marinade ingredients in a large non-reactive bowl. Add lamb pieces and toss well to coat. Cover and marinate in the refrigerator for up to 24 hours.

2 Drain and reserve marinade. Thread 4–5 lamb pieces onto each rosemary stem.

3 Grill over medium-high heat for about 8–10 minutes, turning and basting with reserved marinade frequently. Throw rosemary leaves onto fire and close the grill lid during the last 2–3 minutes of cooking for extra flavor.

4 Serve over rice pilaf.

SCALLOP and MUSSEL kebabs

SERVES 4

Marinade

¼ cup • 50 mL	olive oil
¼ cup • 50 mL	lemon juice
1 Tbsp • 15 mL	finely chopped parsley
1 tsp • 5 mL	garlic paste
1 tsp • 5 mL	ginger paste
1 tsp • 5 mL	red pepper flakes
1 tsp • 5 mL	salt
½ tsp • 2.5 mL	freshly ground black pepper

Kebabs

32	steamed and shucked blue mussels
8	strips Canadian bacon, each strip cut into 4 pieces
24	medium sea scallops
8	medium metal or presoaked bamboo skewers

1. Combine all marinade ingredients in a non-reactive bowl. Add scallops and mussels and toss gently to coat. Cover and marinate in the refrigerator for up to 2 hours.

2. Drain and reserve marinade. Wrap each mussel in a bacon piece. Thread 3 scallops horizontally alternating with 4 bacon wrapped mussels onto each skewer.

3. Grill over medium fire until bacon starts to become crisp, 2–3 minutes per side. Baste each side with reserved marinade once only and grill for another minute.

4. Serve over saffron rice pilaf (recipe page 219) or with salad.

• *Eastern Canada is famous for the Digby scallops of Nova Scotia and cultured blue mussels from Prince Edward Island.*

HALIBUT and SALMON Kebabs

Marinade

¼ cup • 50 mL	olive oil
¼ cup • 50 mL	lemon juice
¼ cup • 50 mL	dry white wine
1 Tbsp • 15 mL	finely chopped fresh dill
1 Tbsp • 15 mL	grated lemon zest
1 tsp • 5 mL	garlic paste
1 tsp • 5 mL	red pepper flakes
1 tsp • 5 mL	sugar
½ tsp • 2.5 mL	salt
½ tsp • 2.5 mL	freshly ground black pepper
	vegetable oil for basting

Kebabs

1 lb • 500 g	sockeye, coho or spring salmon fillet, cut into 1-inch (2.5-cm) cubes
1 lb • 500 g	halibut fillet, cut into 1-inch (2.5-cm) cubes
8	cherry tomatoes
8	medium metal or presoaked wooden skewers

1 Combine all marinade ingredients in a non-reactive bowl. Add fish pieces and toss gently to coat. Cover and marinate in the refrigerator for 2 hours.

2 Drain marinade and reserve. Thread 3–4 pieces of halibut alternating with salmon onto each skewer. Top each skewer with a cherry tomato. Brush liberally with reserved marinade.

3 Grill over medium heat for 2 minutes on each side, turning only once and basting with the marinade. Grill both sides an additional minute, basting liberally at each turn, until both fish are opaque.

4 For a gorgeous colorful presentation, serve over saffron rice pilaf (recipe page 219) garnished with cherry tomatoes.

• *A colorful Pacific Northwest creation combining two popular fish of the Pacific coast.*

JALOU KEBABS

SERVES 4 *Marinade*

¼ cup • 50 mL	jerk paste (recipe page 226)
2 Tbsp • 25 mL	**Cajun spice mix (recipe page 227)**
1 Tbsp • 15 mL	**olive oil**

Kebabs

2 lb • 1 kg	**lean boneless beef, pork or chicken, cut into 1½-inch (4-cm) cubes**
1	**large red onion, cut into 8 sections, and layers separated**
1	**large red bell pepper, seeded and cut into 1½-inch (4-cm) squares**
2	**narrow zucchini, cut crosswise into ½-inch (1-cm) pieces**
8	**long metal or presoaked bamboo skewers**
¼ cup • 50 mL	**vegetable oil mixed with an equal amount of water for basting**

1 Combine ingredients for marinade in a non-reactive bowl. Add meat pieces and toss well to coat each piece thoroughly. Cover and marinate in the refrigerator overnight or up to 24 hours.

2 Thread about 5 meat pieces onto each skewer, alternating with onion, red pepper and zucchini.

3 Grill over medium heat for 4–5 minutes per side, or until cooked, basting with oil and water mixture occasionally. Sprinkle kebabs with salt and pepper.

4 Serve over rice pilaf or with salad of your choice.

• *These kababs combine the complexity of Jamaican jerk marinade with Lousiana's spicy Cajun mixture to impart an extraordinary taste to beef, pork or poultry. I coined the name* Jalou *from the first syllables of Jamaica and Louisiana.*

Thanksgiving TURKEY KEBABS

Marinade

½ cup • 125 mL	white wine
¼ cup • 50 mL	olive oil
¼ cup • 50 mL	lemon juice
1 Tbsp • 15 mL	finely chopped fresh sage
1 Tbsp • 15 mL	finely chopped fresh parsley
1 tsp • 5 mL	dried oregano
1 tsp • 5 mL	salt
½ tsp • 2.5 mL	freshly ground black pepper

Kebabs

1 lb • 500 g	boneless turkey breast cut into 1-inch (2.5-cm) cubes
1 lb • 500 g	boneless turkey thighs, cut into 1-inch (2.5-cm) cubes
24	small boiled Brussels sprouts
24	cherry tomatoes
2	medium narrow zucchini
12	long metal skewers

1 Combine all marinade ingredients and divide the marinade into equal parts in 2 non-reactive bowls. Add turkey breast meat and tomatoes in one and turkey thigh meat and Brussels sprouts in the other bowl. Add turkey pieces, Brussels sprouts and tomatoes. Toss well to coat, cover and let marinate in the refrigerator for up to 6 hours.

2 Drain and reserve marinade.

3 Slice the zucchini lengthwise into strips ¼ inch (0.5 cm) thick. Cut strips into pieces 2½–3 inch (6–7.5 cm) long. Wrap a zucchini slice around each turkey breast piece and thread 5 pieces alternating with 4 cherry tomatoes onto 6 skewers. Thread 5 pieces of thigh meat alternating with 4 Brussels sprouts on the remaining 6 skewers.

4 Grill over medium heat, turning skewers and basting with reserved marinade often. Cook for 6–8 minutes or until meat is cooked.

5 Serve one breast skewer and one thigh skewer per plate. Accompany with traditional mashed potatoes, gravy, seasonal vegetable of your choice and cranberry sauce.

Serve these turkey kebabs instead of cooking a whole turkey and worrying about leftovers. This works well for a couple or for a small group and it can still be served with the traditional accompaniments.

TOFU KEBABS

Marinade

2 Tbsp • 25 mL	*ketjap manis* (sweet soy sauce), (see page 229)
1 Tbsp • 15 mL	oyster sauce
1 Tbsp • 15 mL	sesame oil
1 Tbsp • 15 mL	rice wine vinegar
1 Tbsp • 15 mL	finely chopped cilantro
1. tsp • 5 mL	ginger paste
1 tsp • 5 mL	chili garlic sauce
¼ tsp • 1 mL	five-spice powder

Kebabs

1 lb • 500 g	extra-firm tofu, drained and gently pressed to remove excess moisture, and cut into 1-inch (2.5-cm) cubes
2	narrow zucchini, cut into ½-inch (1-cm) rounds
1	large red bell pepper, seeded and cut into 1-inch (2.5-cm) squares
8	long presoaked wooden skewers
1 tsp • 5 mL	toasted sesame seeds
¼ cup • 50 mL	vegetable oil mixed with an equal amount of water for basting

1 Combine all marinade ingredients in a non-reactive bowl. Add tofu and toss gently to coat. Cover and marinate in the refrigerator for at least 4 hours but preferably overnight.

2 Remove tofu cubes from the marinade. Thread 5–6 pieces of tofu alternating with zucchini and red pepper onto each skewer.

3 Preheat the grill to medium and brush the cooking grid with oil. Grill skewer for 2 minutes. Baste with oil and water mixture and grill for 1 minute longer. Turn skewer and repeat, for a total cooking time of 3 minutes per side.

4 Sprinkle skewers with toasted sesame seeds and serve over rice or with salad.

• *Tofu is not only high in protein, it is also extremely versatile, since it absorbs the flavor from any type of marinade. This recipe uses an Asian-inspired marinade and flavors and was suggested by our friend Rita Bhatia.*

Maple syrup-mustard CHICKEN KEBABS

Marinade

¼ cup • 50 mL	olive oil
¼ cup • 50 mL	maple syrup
2 Tbsp • 25 mL	lemon juice
1 Tbsp • 15 mL	Dijon mustard
1 Tbsp • 15 mL	minced garlic
1 tsp • 5 mL	dried thyme
1 tsp • 5 mL	salt
½ tsp • 2.5 mL	freshly ground black pepper
½ tsp • 2.5 mL	dried mustard

Kebabs

1½ lb • 750 g	chicken breast, cut into 1-inch (2.5-cm) cubes
1	large red onion, cut into 1½-inch (4-cm) wedges
1	large red bell pepper, seeded and cut into 1-inch (2.5-cm) squares
1	large yellow bell pepper, seeded and cut into 1-inch (2.5–cm) squares
8	medium metal or presoaked bamboo skewers

1 Combine all marinade ingredients in a non-reactive bowl. Add chicken pieces and toss well to coat. Cover and marinate for at least 6 hours in the refrigerator.

2 Remove chicken and reserve marinade. Thread about 4–5 pieces of chicken alternating with onion and red and yellow peppers onto each skewer.

3 Grill over medium heat for 3–4 minutes per side, turning and basting with marinade frequently.

4 Serve with saffron rice pilaf (recipe page 219) or salad of your choice.

Oceania

This region includes such diverse places as Australia, New Zealand, the South Pacific and Hawaii, all of which offer their own unique cuisines and cooking styles.

In the past Australia suffered from a reputation of notoriously dull and uninspiring national cuisine. Settled by the British some 200 years ago, it was used initially as a penal colony and its cuisine was dominated by English-style cooking. After the Second World War, Australia, still adhering to its white Australia policy, encouraged European settlement. Waves of immigrants, mainly from Greece, Italy, Spain, Germany and Yugoslavia, made Australia their home. After 1970 Australia dropped its white immigration policy and immigrants began to arrive from the Middle East, Eastern Europe and other diverse areas. The immigration policy was further liberalized and Asian immigrants from China, Japan, Korea, Southeast Asia, the Indian subcontinent and Africa started arriving from 1980 onward.

These diverse groups brought radical changes to the Australian culinary landscape. Local chefs defied traditional cooking rules and started mixing foods, flavors and cooking styles from other ethnic groups. Contemporary Australian cuisine is a hybrid that reflects the country's multi-ethnic and multicultural makeup, along with the variety, quality and abundance of local fruits, vegetables, meats and seafood. Today's cuisine also incorporates foods that Aborigines depended on for centuries. Dubbed the "bush tucker" cuisine, it includes items such as crocodile meat, many varieties of fish and shellfish, and nuts and fruits gathered in the bush to create a blend of tastes and textures found only in Australia.

Outdoor cooking is a way of life in Australia and most Australians like a casual lifestyle. Most homes have some sort of barbecue and, because of the availability of excellent meat, fresh fish and seafood, not to mention generally favorable weather, Australians prefer to cook outdoors on their grills. Since most Australians live along the coast, they have access to abundant and varied fresh fish and shellfish. The kebab culture is well established in Australia and has gone beyond " shrimps on the barbie" to include kebabs made from exotic meats such as kangaroo, crocodile, emu, ostrich and camel, as well as traditional lamb, beef, pork, goat, poultry, tuna and squid.

With the increasing contribution of other ethnic groups, such as Lebanese, Greeks, Turks, Indians,

Indonesians, Thais, Malays, Vietnamese, Japanese and Koreans, kebabs have become the most popular fast food in Australia. In Melbourne souvlaki is king because of a concentration of Greek immigrants in that city; Sydney has its ubiquitous doner kebab; and Hobart and Cairns favor seafood kebabs.

Charcoal-grilled kangaroo kebabs, sometimes referred to as roo kebabs or kanga kebabs, are uniquely Australian. Kangaroo has a mild gamey flavor, and is very low in fat and rich in protein and other nutrients. It is a standard item on the menu of some top restaurants in Australia. Being low in fat it is prone to drying out during grilling and is generally presoaked in oil before cooking or treated with marinades with a high oil content.

With over 10 million sheep to every person, New Zealand produces an enormous quantity of lamb meat, a substantial portion of which finds its way into markets around the world. The kebab culture in New Zealand is alive and expanding, thanks to an influx of immigrants of Turkish origin and those from the Mediterranean countries where lamb and seafood are preferred. Takeout kebab outlets are a common sight and compete quite successfully with pizza joints, Chinese restaurants and Indian eateries in Auckland, Wellington and Christchurch.

The cuisine of French Polynesia reflects French, Chinese and Italian culinary influences but the cooking style still retains its old South Pacific characteristic of using traditional pit ovens, called *ahimaa*, for slow cooking of food wrapped in banana leaves. Five island groups make up French Polynesia. Tahiti is the biggest and most famous island and Papeete, its capital, has several good restaurants serving mostly French, Chinese and Polynesian specialties. Kebabs are also popular but they are only sold from *les roulottes*, trucks parked along the waterfront. *Les roulottes* are colorfully painted and brightly lit food vans that line up at the Papeete waterfront at sundown and sell a variety of foods from pizza to crêpes, and including brochettes or shish kebabs. In the evening locals and visitors throng Vaiete Square and buy Chinese, Italian, French, Tahitian and Vietnamese food from the food vans as a pleasant and inexpensive treat. Freshly grilled brochettes or kebabs of pork, chicken or fresh fish served with chips are a hot seller.

Elsewhere in the South Pacific, kebabs are not part of the main diet; although a few outlets are run by expatriates and generally cater to tourists. Contemporary Fijian cuisine is a fusion of Polynesian, Melanesian, Indian, Chinese and European cuisines reflecting the many diverse ethnic groups that make up the Fijian population. Kebabs are not a common item on restaurant menus in Fiji, but they are available in some restaurants.

They are likely to be seasoned with East Indian spices and cooked East Indian-style because East Indians are the largest ethnic group here. Some of the resort hotels in Fiji that are popular with Australians do make an attempt to make their guests feel at home by laying on an Australian-style barbecue with all varieties of seafood kebabs. In Port Moresby, the capital of Papua New Guinea, which occupies the eastern half of New Guinea, hotel restaurants serve Asian and European cuisine. Traditional cuisine is based on root vegetables, pork and rice, but unusual kebabs made from local delicacies like crocodile meat or sago grubs add to the culinary scene.

Different parts of Asia, Europe, Polynesia and the U.S. mainland have all contributed to the rich and varied Hawaiian cuisine often referred to as *hapa*. It has embraced the foods of Samoa, Japan, China, Korea, the Philippines, Puerto Rico, North America, France, Portugal and Britain to create a vibrant culinary fusion. For some unexplainable reason, pineapples are associated with Hawaiian cuisine and the addition of pineapple to a dish is supposed to transform it into a Hawaiian culinary delight. Perhaps the fact that Dole's pineapples are Hawaii's main export has something to do with it. However, Hawaiian cuisine is more than pineapples and more than the traditional luau food and plate lunches. The new generation of Hawaiian chefs relies on a wide variety of local fresh fish, seafood and meats cooked with Asian spices and herbs, sauces and mixed with fresh exotic fruits and nuts. Kebabs are sold in hotel restaurants catering to tourists but a street vendor selling kebabs is a rare sight on the islands of Hawaii. When available, the kebabs lean toward pork, shrimp and fish alternating with fresh fruits.

SHRIMP on the BARBIE

SERVES 4

Marinade

¼ cup • 50 mL	olive oil
¼ cup • 50 mL	lemon juice
2 Tbsp • 25 mL	finely chopped fresh parsley
2 Tbsp • 25 mL	finely chopped fresh thyme
2 Tbsp • 25 mL	finely chopped fresh cilantro
1 tsp • 5 mL	garlic paste
1 tsp • 5 mL	chili sauce
1 tsp • 5 mL	salt
1 tsp • 5 mL	dried oregano
½ tsp • 2.5 mL	freshly ground black pepper

Kebabs

24	extra large shrimp (16–20 count), shelled and deveined
8	medium metal or presoaked bamboo skewers
¼ cup • 50 mL	melted butter for basting

1. Combine all marinade ingredients in a bowl. Add shrimp and toss. Cover and marinate in the refrigerator for up to 4 hours.

2. Remove shrimp from marinade and thread 3 shrimps onto each skewer.

3. Grill over medium heat for 2–3 minutes per side or until shrimp are pink and cooked through. Be careful not to overcook them.

4. Remove from heat, brush with melted butter and serve immediately on a bed of spinach garnished with lemon wedges.

- *The most famous Australian barbecue recipe, shrimp marinated with a variety of marinades and grilled outdoors, is an Australian social tradition.*

TOFU KEBABS   page 202

MAPLE SYRUP-MUSTARD CHICKEN KEBABS   page 203

SHRIMP ON THE BARBIE   page 208

HAWAIIAN SEAFOOD KEBABS   page 214

Snags on the Barbie

12	**Australian sausages**
2	**medium onions, cut into 8 wedges**
12	**medium metal or presoaked bamboo skewers**

1 Boil sausages in a pan for about 5 minutes. Remove and prick all over with a fine skewer. Cut each sausage into 2-inch (5-cm) pieces.

2 Thread 2–3 sausage pieces, alternating with onion wedges onto each skewer.

3 Grill over medium heat for 3–5 minutes per side, or until sausage is golden brown and the onion slightly charred.

4 Serve skewers brushed with a hot sauce (optional) and accompanied by a cold beer.

- *A favorite Aussie expression is "Pop over, we'll chuck a few snags on the barbie and crack a few stubbies." Meaning, you are invited to have some grilled sausages washed down with a beer. Snags are Australian sausages and a must for barbecuing.*

£AMB KEBABS with kiwi fruit

SERVES 4

Marinade

1	kiwi fruit, flesh scooped out and minced
¼ cup • 50 mL	dry red wine
2 Tbsp • 25 mL	soy sauce
2 Tbsp • 25 mL	vegetable or olive oil
2 Tbsp • 25 mL	sweet sherry
1 tsp • 5 mL	garlic paste
1 tsp • 5 mL	ginger paste
½ tsp • 2.5 mL	freshly ground black pepper

Kebabs

2 lb • 1 kg	boneless lamb shoulder cut into 1 inch (2.5 cm) cubes
8	medium metal or presoaked bamboo skewers

1 In a bowl combine all marinade ingredients. Add lamb and toss well to coat thoroughly. Cover and marinate in the refrigerator for up to 24 hours.

2 Drain and reserve marinade. If marination exceeds 12 hours, boil reserved marinade for at least 2 minutes. Thread 5–6 pieces of lamb onto each skewer leaving ¼-inch (0.5 cm) space between them.

3 Grill over medium-high heat for 6–8 minutes or until cooked, turning and basting with reserved marinade often.

4 Serve over rice pilaf.

LAMB SATAY

Marinade

½ cup • 125 mL	red wine
¼ cup • 50 mL	olive or vegetable oil
1 Tbsp • 15 mL	lemon juice
1 Tbsp • 15 mL	finely chopped cilantro
1 tsp • 5 mL	minced garlic
½ tsp • 2.5 mL	salt
½ tsp • 2.5 mL	freshly ground black pepper

Kebabs

1 lb • 500 g	lamb fillet or loin cut into strips 3 inch (7.5 cm) long, ¾ inch (2 cm) wide and ¼ inch (0.5 cm) thick
12	medium presoaked bamboo skewers

1 Mix all marinade ingredients in a bowl. Add lamb strips, cover and marinate for up to 4 hours at room temperature or overnight in the refrigerator.

2 Drain marinade and reserve. Thread each lamb strip onto a skewer.

3 Grill over medium-high heat for about 3 minutes per side, turning and basting frequently with reserved marinade.

4 Serve with mint sauce or chutney.

Green MUSSEL KEBABS

The bountiful coastal waters of New Zealand are the source of excellent green mussels through aquaculture. This recipe captures the texture and subtle flavors of the bacon-wrapped kebabs I tried in a Christchurch restaurant.

SERVES 4

Marinade

½ cup • 125 mL	**white wine**
2 Tbsp • 25 mL	**olive oil**
2 Tbsp • 25 mL	**lemon or lime juice**
1 Tbsp • 15 mL	**finely chopped fresh dill**
1 Tbsp • 15 mL	**honey**
1 tsp • 5 mL	**minced garlic**

Kebabs

32	**steamed and shucked green mussels**
8	**strips of bacon, each cut into 4 sections**
8	**medium presoaked wooden skewers**

1 Combine marinade ingredients in a non-reactive bowl. Add mussel meat, toss and marinate for an hour.

2 Remove mussels from marinade and pat dry with a paper towel. Wrap each mussel in a bacon piece.

3 Thread 4 wrapped mussels onto each skewer.

4 Grill over medium heat until the bacon becomes crisp, 3–4 minutes.

5 Serve as an appetizer, garnished with lemon wedges.

Skewered COCONUT SHRIMP

Ono Nui Shrimp

In Hawaiian *ono nui* means "very good." This recipe does not involve grilling; shrimp are first coated with coconut and then deep-fried.

SERVES 6
AS AN APPETIZER

½ cup • 125 mL	**all-purpose flour**
½ tsp • 2.5 mL	**salt**
1½ cups • 375 mL	**shredded unsweetened coconut**
2	**eggs, beaten with a pinch of salt**
1 lb • 500 g	**large shrimp (16–20 count), deveined and peeled except tail**
6	**long presoaked wooden skewers**
	oil for deep-frying

1   Mix flour with salt in a large shallow dish.

2   Place shredded coconut and beaten eggs in separate shallow dishes.

3   Thread 3–4 shrimp onto each skewer. Roll the skewers in seasoned flour, then in beaten egg and finally in shredded coconut. Ensure that each shrimp is fully coated with coconut.

4   Deep-fry the skewers in vegetable oil heated to 350°F (180°C) until shrimp turn golden brown, 3–4 minutes.

5   Drain skewers on paper towel and serve immediately with a sweet dipping sauce of your choice.

Hawaiian SEAFOOD KEBABS

SERVES 6

Marinade

¼ cup • 50 mL	dry sherry
¼ cup • 50 mL	sake
2 Tbsp • 25 mL	sesame oil
2 Tbsp • 25 mL	grated ginger
1 Tbsp • 15 mL	minced garlic
1 Tbsp • 15 mL	lime juice
2 tsp • 10 mL	soy sauce

Kebabs

1 lb • 500 g	sea scallops
1 lb • 500 g	large shrimp (21–30 count), shelled and deveined
2	green bell peppers, seeded and cut into 1½-inch (4-cm) squares
1	medium red onion, cut into 1½-inch (4-cm) wedges
1	fresh pineapple, cut into 1-inch (2.5-cm) cubes
6	long metal or presoaked wooden skewers

1 Mix all marinade ingredients in a non-reactive bowl. Add scallops and shrimp and toss gently to coat. Marinate for 2 hours in the refrigerator.

2 Remove seafood from the marinade and reserve marinade. Thread scallops and shrimps alternating with green pepper, onion and pineapple onto each skewer.

3 Grill over medium heat for 5–7 minutes, turning skewers frequently and basting with reserved marinade.

4 Serve over rice as a main course, or as an appetizer without rice.

PORK and PINEAPPLE kebabs

Marinade

¼ cup • 50 mL	pineapple juice
¼ cup • 50 mL	olive oil or vegetable oil
2 Tbsp • 25 mL	hoisin sauce
1 tsp • 5 mL	Dijon mustard
1 tsp • 5 mL	grated fresh ginger
1 tsp • 5 mL	red pepper flakes

Kebabs

1 lb • 500 g	lean boneless pork cut into 1-inch (2.5-cm) cubes
½	fresh pineapple cut into ¾-inch (2-cm) cubes
1	green or red bell pepper, seeded and cut into 1-inch (2.5-cm) squares
8	medium presoaked bamboo skewers

1 Combine all marinade ingredients in a non-reactive bowl. Add pork and toss to coat. Cover and marinate in the refrigerator for at least 1 hour and not more than 3 hours.

2 Remove pork, reserving marinade. Thread 3–4 pork pieces alternating with pepper and pineapple onto each skewer.

3 Grill over medium-high heat for 8–10 minutes or until pork is no longer pink in the center, turning skewers occasionally and basting with reserved marinade.

4 Serve over rice pilaf.

Kebab
Accompaniments

No kebab preparation is complete without the appropriate accompaniments. These accompaniments are meant not only to complement and supplement the kebabs, but also to enhance the taste and appearance. One rule worth remembering is to keep the accompaniments simple and light so they do not overwhelm the kebabs, which should remain the centerpiece of the meal. Each country or region has its own favorite accompaniments to serve with kebabs and they generally fall into one or more of the following categories.

SIDE DISHES

Rice pilaf is the most popular side dish generally served with kebabs. Also known as *pilav, pilau, pilaf, plov, pulao, pullaw, palow, polo, polov* and *polow* in different countries, it can be a simple rice preparation or an elaborate one cooked with spices, herbs, meats and vegetables. Although there are several varieties of pilafs, my favorite is saffron pilaf (recipe page 219) not only because of its bright yellow color but also because of its subtle flavor that complements the kebabs. Another popular side dish served with kebabs is risotto—a traditional Italian preparation made from toasted rice cooked with hot chicken, beef or seafood stock and an optional assortment of flavorings. Risotto is popular in Northern Italy and is a mainstay of Milanese cooking.

Side dishes made from grains other than rice are also served with kebabs. In Armenia and some Middle Eastern countries, bulgar is substituted for rice in pilaf. Bulgar is a type of wheat that has been steamed and dried. It needs little or no cooking and can be used in hot cereals, rolls and salads.

Polenta, an extremely versatile and popular dish in northern Italy, is eaten with all types of foods, including kebabs. It is a coarsely ground cornmeal boiled with water or stock to obtain a creamy consistency.

A staple of Morocco and other neighboring North African countries, couscous is considered a healthy alternative to rice and is easier and quicker to cook. It is a coarsely ground semolina pasta with a pleasing texture and a subtle nutty taste.

SALADS

A variety of salads are commonly served with kebabs, the main ingredients being lettuce, sliced tomatoes, cucumber and raw onion. Fresh lemon or lime juice is preferred over vinegar when serving salad with kebabs. In some countries pasta salad, Asian noodle salad or potato salad is served with grilled meat.

Other places go for grilled vegetable salad with its crunchy texture and charred smoky flavor. Salads are a perfect accompaniment to kebabs—they are light, nutritious and colorful and no prior cooking is required.

BREADS

Each country or region has its own traditional bread that goes well with its characteristic kebab preparation. There is pita bread (Greece), *pide* (Turkey), *lavash* (Iran), *naan* (India), *ksra* (Morocco), *khoubiz* (the Middle East) and *lipioshka* (Central Asia) (see also glossary, pages 228–31).

SAUCES AND CONDIMENTS

Sauces and condiments come in many varieties and are meant to add flavor, taste, complexity and visual appeal to kebabs. They can be simply accompanying sauces such as peanut sauce (recipe page 220) served with satays or a variety of dipping sauces used with Vietnamese, Thai and Japanese skewered grilled foods. Sweetened barbecue-style sauces enhance the taste and appearance of cooked meat and are applied just prior to or soon after grilling.

Commonly used sauces served with kebabs in different countries include charmoula (Morocco, recipe page 221), harissa (North Africa, recipe page 224), chimichurri (Argentina, recipe page 223), nuoc cham (Vietnam), adobo (Latin America, recipe page 225), ketjap manis (Indonesia) and tzatziki (Greece, recipe page 222). Condiments, pickles, chutneys, relish and salsa are also served with kebabs and there are no hard or fast rules as to what goes with a particular kebab.

SPICES AND SPICE BLENDS

These are generally dry mixtures of the various spices and herbs meant to season and perk up meat and vegetable dishes. Different countries have their own characteristic spice mixtures that are either incorporated into the food while cooking or just sprinkled over the cooked food. Notable spice and spice blends are *baharat* (Middle East and North Africa), *Ras el-hanout* (Morocco), *garam masala* (South Asia, recipe page 227), *sumac* (Turkey) and *piri piri* (Portugal). (See also glossary, pages 228–31.)

Recipes for Some Common
KEBAB ACCOMPANIMENTS

SAFFRON RICE PILAF

¼ tsp • 0.5 mL	**saffron**
1½ cups • 375 mL	**warm water**
1 cup • 250 mL	**basmati rice**
1 Tbsp • 15 mL	**olive oil**
1 Tbsp • 15 mL	**finely chopped onion**
1 tsp • 5 mL	**garlic paste**
1 tsp • 5 mL	**salt**

1 Add saffron to 1½ cups (375 mL) warm water, stir and cover. Let rest for 2–3 hours or until water turns bright yellow.

2 Wash rice thoroughly. Soak in 2–3 cups of cold water for 30 minutes.

3 In a pan heat oil over medium heat and sauté onion until translucent, 2–3 minutes. Add garlic paste and fry for exactly 1 minute. Remove pan from heat.

4 Drain rice and transfer to pan. Mix well to incorporate sautéed onion and garlic into rice. Add saffron water and salt to rice, bring to boil, cover, reduce heat and simmer at lowest setting for 15–20 minutes.

5 Fluff the rice with a fork and serve.

peanut sauce (malaysia/singapore style)

Make this peanut sauce a day before in order to develop its full flavor.
Warm the sauce before serving.

MAKES APPROX.
1½ cups (375 ml)

2 Tbsp • 25 mL	vegetable oil	
1	medium onion, finely chopped	
1 tsp • 5 mL	garlic paste	
1 tsp • 5 mL	ginger paste	
⅔ cup • 150 mL	unsweetened crunchy peanut butter	
⅓ cup • 75 mL	coconut milk	
¼ cup • 50 mL	chopped cilantro	
¼ cup • 50 mL	lime juice	
¼ cup • 50 mL	soy sauce	
1	stalk lemon grass, finely chopped	
1 Tbsp • 15 mL	brown sugar	
1 tsp • 5 mL	chili paste	
1 tsp • 5 mL	ground turmeric	

1 In a pan, heat oil and sauté onion till soft.

2 Add ginger and garlic paste, fry for 1 minute.

3 Add chili paste, lime juice, peanut butter, sugar, soy sauce, lemon grass, turmeric and coconut milk. Mix well and continue cooking mixture on low to medium heat for 10 minutes.

4 Remove from heat and stir in cilantro leaves. Adjust salt and sugar to taste.

CHARMOULA SAUCE

This is a versatile sauce and can be used as a marinade as well as a sauce.

MAKES APPROX.
1 CUP (250 ML)

¼ cup • 50 mL	olive oil
¼ cup • 50 mL	lemon juice
½ cup • 125 mL	finely chopped cilantro leaves
½ cup • 125 mL	finely chopped parsley
2 Tbsp • 25 mL	ground cumin
2 tsp • 10 mL	paprika
1	hot red chili, seeded (optional)
½ tsp • 2.5 mL	ground ginger
½ tsp • 2.5 mL	dried marjoram
½ tsp • 2.5 mL	freshly ground black pepper
½ tsp • 2.5 mL	salt

1 Combine all the ingredients in a food processor and blend until a smooth paste is obtained. Adjust the seasoning; if a hotter version is required, add cayenne pepper according to taste.

2 Store in a jar in the refrigerator until needed.

TZATZIKI

½	long English cucumber
1 cup • 250 mL	strained plain yogurt
1 Tbsp • 15 mL	minced garlic
1 Tbsp • 15 mL	chopped fresh dill or mint
1 tsp • 5 mL	lemon juice
½ tsp • 2.5 mL	salt
½ tsp • 2.5 mL	freshly ground black pepper
¼ tsp • 1 mL	onion powder
1 Tbsp • 15 mL	olive oil

1 Grate cucumber along with its skin. Remove most of its water by placing in a cheesecloth and squeezing hard.

2 Mix grated cucumber with yogurt. Add garlic, dill, lemon juice, salt, pepper and onion powder and stir well.

3 Stir in olive oil and refrigerate for at least 2 hours for flavors to blend.

4 To serve, top with extra slices of cucumber and mint leaves. Serve either chilled or at room temperature. The sauce keeps in the refrigerator for up to 1 week.

CHIMICHURRI

1 cup • 250 mL	cilantro leaves
¼ cup • 50 mL	fresh Italian parsley
2 Tbsp • 25 mL	lemon juice
1 Tbsp • 15 mL	red wine vinegar
1 Tbsp • 15 mL	minced garlic
2	green hot chilies, seeded
1 tsp • 5 mL	salt
1 tsp • 5 mL	dried oregano
½ tsp • 2.5 mL	ground cumin
½ tsp • 2.5 mL	freshly ground black pepper
⅓ cup • 75 mL	olive oil

1 In a food processor, blend cilantro, parsley, lemon juice, vinegar, garlic, chilies, oregano, cumin, salt and pepper to a smooth paste.

2 With food processor running, gradually add olive oil and let the paste absorb it. Adjust seasoning, if required.

3 Use immediately or refrigerate until ready to use.

HARISSA

6	dried hot red chilies, seeded
4	garlic cloves
⅓ cup • 75 mL	olive oil
3 Tbsp • 45 mL	paprika
2 Tbsp • 25 mL	hot water
1 tsp • 5 mL	ground roasted coriander seeds
1 tsp • 5 mL	ground roasted cumin seeds
1 tsp • 5 mL	ground caraway seeds
1 tsp • 5 mL	salt

1 Soak dried chilies in hot water for 5–10 minutes to soften.

2 Transfer chilies and other ingredients to blender. Process until mixture forms a smooth paste. Add more water or oil if necessary to ensure a proper consistency.

3 Transfer paste to a jar, cover with thin film of olive oil and store in refrigerator until needed.

ADOBO SAUCE

3	dried chipotle or ancho chilies, seeded
¼ cup • 50 mL	lime juice
¼ cup • 50 mL	vinegar
¼ cup • 50 mL	orange juice
3 Tbsp • 45 mL	tomato paste
1 tsp • 5 mL	dried oregano
1 tsp • 5 mL	ground cumin
½ tsp • 2.5 mL	freshly ground black pepper
¼ cup • 50 mL	vegetable oil
1	medium onion, finely chopped
1 tsp • 5 mL	minced garlic

1 Soak dried chilies in hot water for 15 minutes to soften.

2 Transfer softened chilies, lime juice, vinegar, orange juice, tomato paste, oregano, cumin and pepper to a food processor. Process until a smooth paste is obtained.

3 In a pan heat oil and sauté onion over medium heat until translucent. Add garlic and fry only for 1 minute. Add paste to onion-garlic mixture and cook for about 10 minutes over medium heat.

4 Cool and store in refrigerator for up to 1 week. This sauce can also be used as a marinade.

JERK PASTE

For a hotter version add 2 seeded scotch bonnet or jalapeño peppers while blending.
Use 2 Tbsp (25 mL) jerk paste for each pound (500 g) of meat.

MAKES APPROX.
1 CUP (250 ML)

1	medium onion, coarsely chopped
2	green onions, coarsely chopped
3 Tbsp • 45 mL	soy sauce
2 Tbsp • 25 mL	white vinegar
2 Tbsp • 25 mL	lime juice
2 Tbsp • 25 mL	dark rum
2 Tbsp • 25 mL	brown sugar
2 tsp • 10 mL	freshly ground black pepper
1 tsp • 5 mL	garlic paste
1 tsp • 5 mL	ginger paste
1 tsp • 5 mL	dried sage
1 tsp • 5 mL	dried allspice
1 tsp • 5 mL	dried thyme
1 tsp • 5 mL	hot red pepper flakes
1 tsp • 5 mL	salt
½ tsp • 2.5 mL	ground cinnamon
½ tsp • 2.5 mL	ground nutmeg
3 Tbsp • 45 mL	olive oil

1 Process all ingredients, except olive oil, in a blender. When a smooth purée forms, gradually add olive oil and continue blending until a smooth paste is obtained.

2 Cover and store in a jar in the refrigerator until needed.

GARAM MASALA

CAJUN SPICE MIX

2	2-inch (5-cm) long cinnamon sticks
2 Tbsp • 25 mL	cumin seeds
1 Tbsp • 15 mL	black peppercorns
1½ tsp • 7.5 mL	whole cloves
6	large black cardamom pods (shell removed)
12	green cardamom pods (shell removed)
½ tsp • 2.5 mL	ground mace
½ tsp • 2.5 mL	ground nutmeg

1 Tbsp • 15 mL	paprika
2½ tsp • 12 mL	salt
1 tsp • 5 mL	onion powder
1 tsp • 5 mL	cayenne pepper
1 tsp • 5 mL	ground cumin
1 tsp • 5 mL	ground black pepper
1 tsp • 5 mL	ground white pepper
½ tsp • 2.5 mL	dried thyme
½ tsp • 2.5 mL	dried oregano

1 Grind all the above ingredients in a coffee grinder until a fine powder is obtained.

2 Store in an airtight jar.

1 Mix together all the above ingredients.

2 Store in an airtight jar.

GLOSSARY

Adobo: Adobo sauce is Mexican in origin but popular throughout Latin America and the Caribbean. A piquant sauce or paste made from chilies, herbs, vinegar, garlic and tomato paste, it goes great with beef, poultry and fish preparations. It is used both as a sauce and as a marinade (recipe page 225).

Ajad: Thai fresh pickle made of chopped cucumber, rice vinegar, red or green chilies, sugar and salt. Chopped shallots and chopped carrots are often added. Available at Oriental food stores.

Baharat: An aromatic spice blend of black peppercorn, coriander seeds, cinnamon, cloves, cumin, cardamom, nutmeg, paprika and cassia bark. Used in Middle Eastern and North African countries to perk up meat and vegetable dishes and couscous. Available in Middle Eastern food stores.

Charmoula: A bright green Moroccan sauce made of fresh cilantro and parsley, lemon juice, olive oil, cumin, garlic and chilies. It is a versatile sauce and can be used as a dip, vinaigrette or marinade. Goes well with fish and chicken dishes (recipe page 221).

Chelou: A Persian spicy buttered rice preparation that is either boiled or baked until it forms a golden crunchy crust at the bottom called *tahdig* which is considered the tastiest part of the dish and is served separately. Chelou is a favorite accompaniment for Iranian kebabs and stews.

Chimichurri: A popular garlicky sauce from Argentina that is served with grilled meat and poultry. Its basic ingredients are cilantro or parsley, vinegar, chilies, cumin and garlic, but there are numerous variations and it is often used as a marinade. Commercially made sauce is available in stores that sell Latin American foods (recipe page 223).

Choreg: Also spelled *choerag*, this is a traditional Armenian sweetbread made on festive occasions. This term is often confused with *churek* which is a flat Armenian bread with sesame seeds.

Eeish baladi: An Egyptian whole wheat flatbread that is used to scoop up all kinds of foods. This soft textured bread is used when serving kebabs.

Galangal: A ginger-like root that is extensively used in Indonesian, Malaysian and Thai cooking. It is similar to ginger but more intense and aromatic. Galangal is available in Chinese, Vietnamese or Indonesian food stores.

Garam masala: A common spice mixture used in the Indian subcontinent to season curries, rice, vegetable and meat preparations. It is highly aromatic and consists of black pepper, cinnamon, cloves, black and green cardamom, cumin and nutmeg. It is available in large supermarkets or East Indian food stores (recipe page 227).

Harissa: This fiery spice paste is used both as a table condiment and as an ingredient in Tunisian and Moroccan cooking. It is made of chilies, garlic, cumin, salt, olive oil and tomatoes and is usually served with couscous. Commercially produced harissa is available in specialty stores or Middle Eastern food stores (recipe page 224).

Kaffir lime: Kaffir lime leaves are an essential ingredient in Thai cooking and add a refreshing flavor to Thai soups and curries. They are widely used in Laotian and Cambodian cuisines and to a lesser extent in Indonesian and Malaysian dishes. They are available frozen or dried in oriental food markets.

Ketjap manis: Also spelled *kecap manis*, this is an Indonesian sweet soy sauce that is dark, syrupy and rich. It is used as a marinade, an ingredient in Indonesian cooking and a table condiment. Made of soy sauce, palm sugar, molasses, galangal and spices, it is sold in bottles at Asian food stores.

Ketupat: A savory compressed rice cake that is wrapped in a woven coconut, palm or banana leaf casing and is normally served with satays in Singapore, Malaysia and Indonesia. Some oriental food stores carry this item.

Khoubiz: A Lebanese flatbread, somewhat similar to pita bread. It is a traditional unleavened bread served with most meals and is popular not only in Lebanon, but also in Syria, Jordan, Iraq and the Gulf States.

Kimchi: An important Korean relish, it is basically made of fermented cabbage to which salt, chilies, garlic, salt fish and seasonings are added to produce a salty, spicy and pungent concoction that adds zest to any food. It is served as a side dish with almost every meal. Available in oriental food stores.

Ksra: A tasty Moroccan traditional bread that is served with spicy Moroccan dishes, particularly with tagine, a spicy Moroccan stew. It is flavored with anise seeds and is often served with kebabs.

Lavash: A large, thin, flat Middle Eastern bread that is available either crispy or soft. It is considered the Armenian national bread but is also popular in Georgia and Iran. It is sold in large rectangular pieces in stores specializing in Middle Eastern foods.

Lemon grass: An important ingredient in Thai and Vietnamese cooking, it is also used in other Southeast Asian countries. It is an aromatic plant that imparts a light lemon flavor to foods. Although the entire stalk of lemon grass is fragrant, usually only the bulb part is minced and used. Available in supermarkets and Asian food stores.

Lipioshka: A round unleavened flatbread from Central Asia, particularly popular in Uzbekistan and Turkmenistan. It is served with lamb kebabs throughout Central Asia.

Mattoua: The Algerian version of Moroccan *ksra* bread, it looks and tastes the same.

Naan: A leavened Indian bread traditionally baked in a tandoor oven. Similar oven-baked breads in different countries are called *naan* (Afghanistan), *nan* (Iran), *non* (Central Asia) and *nang* (China). Freshly baked *naan* goes well with curries and kebabs.

Nam chim pla: A Thai satay dipping sauce made of peanut sauce *(nam chim)* diluted with fish sauce to give it a liquid consistency. Available in some Oriental food stores.

Nam thaeng kwa: A Thai relish that is a traditional accompaniment to many Thai dishes and made of cucumber mixed with vinegar, sugar, chopped peanuts, chilies, lime juice, fish sauce and cilantro. Available in Oriental food stores.

Narsharab: A sweet and sour sauce made from pomegranate juice. It is popular in Azerbaijan and Armenia and is a must with sturgeon kebabs. It is also used as a table sauce or as a marinade for grilled meats. Available in some stores where Iranian and Middle Eastern food is sold.

Nuoc cham: A popular Vietnamese dipping sauce made of dried red chilies, garlic, sugar, fish sauce, vinegar or lemon juice. Variations of this sauce are found in Cambodia, Thailand and the Philippines. Available in Oriental food stores.

Nuoc mam: Also referred to as *nuoc nam*, it is a fermented fish sauce made of anchovies and salt, and is an important ingredient in Vietnamese cooking. It has a strong, pungent and salty taste and is used as both a condiment and flavoring. Available in stores where Oriental food is sold.

Nuoc mam cham: A Vietnamese dipping sauce consisting of rice vinegar, coconut juice, sugar, lime juice, fish sauce, garlic and red chilies. Available in Oriental food stores.

Nuoc mam toi ot: A Vietnamese sweet and hot sauce made of sugar, vinegar, fish sauce, chili-garlic sauce, crushed red peppers and lime juice. Available in Oriental food stores.

Pan criollo: A traditional Puerto Rican bread which looks very similar to French baguette. Puerto Rican kebabs *(pinchos)* are served on it.

Pao: Means bread in Portuguese. There are several varieties of *pao* to be found in Portugal and its ex-colonies, including Brazil.

Pide: The traditional bread that is almost always served with Turkish kebabs. It is a flatbread, but unlike pita bread, does not have a pocket. *Pide* is brushed with olive oil or melted butter, then slightly grilled before serving. It is sold in stores specializing in Greek or Middle Eastern foods.

Pincho powder: A Puerto Rican spice blend made of saffron, Spanish paprika, dried parsley, dried chives, sea salt, dried onion flakes, garlic flakes, chili powder, ground cumin, ground coriander, dried oregano and black pepper. It is used to season Puerto Rican kebabs.

Piri piri: Correctly identified as "Molho de Piri Piri," it is a Portuguese hot pepper sauce. made from olive oil, sea salt, wine vinegar, garlic, oregano and red chilies. It is a traditional table sauce, somewhat like Tabasco, available in restaurants throughout Portugal, as well as in some supermarkets selling ethnic foods.

Raita: A yogurt-based sauce or a side salad popular throughout the Indian subcontinent. It can include an array of vegetables, such as cucumber, tomatoes, onion, eggplant and potato, flavored with roasted ground cumin and mustard seeds, chili powder, salt, mint or cilantro. Raitas are served chilled and have a cooling effect when served with hot spicy foods.

Ras el-hanout: A Moroccan spice blend consisting of ground black pepper, nutmeg, mace, allspice, cinnamon, ginger, fennel, paprika, bay leaves, cayenne pepper, cumin, turmeric and salt. It is used as a seasoning in many Moroccan meat and vegetable dishes. Sold in Middle Eastern food shops.

Roti: A non-leavened whole wheat Indian flatbread eaten daily all across the Indian subcontinent. It is also popular in some parts of the Caribbean, Africa and Southeast Asia among the native population, having been introduced by the Indian settlers. Also referred to as *chapatti*, it is eaten with curried dishes.

Sambal kachang: Sambal generally means a hot chili condiment or a sauce, and there is an infinite variety. *Sambal kachang* refers to a satay sauce made of peanuts, chilies, sugar, onion, garlic, vinegar, tomato paste and shrimp paste. It is a Singaporean and Malaysian speciality and is available in some Oriental food stores.

Sambal kecap or *ketjap:* The sweet chili sauce of Indonesia. It is made from sweet soy sauce *(ketjap manis)* to which chili, shallots, garlic, lemon or lime juice are added. Used as a relish to perk up Indonesian dishes or as a dipping sauce for satays. You can find it in Oriental food stores.

Sambal oelek: Also known as *sambal ulek*, it is a fiery hot Indonesian relish made of red chilies, vinegar or tamarind, shrimp paste, sugar and salt. This relish is added to provide heat to a dish without altering other flavors. Also popular in Malaysia and Thailand. Available in Oriental food stores.

Sangak: The most traditional bread of Iran. It is flat with a pebbly appearance and can be up to 2 feet (30 cm) long. It is widely eaten in Iran and southern Azerbaijan with traditional foods, including kebabs.

Schichimi: Also known as *shichimi togarashi*, this is a Japanese peppery blend of 7 spices, the main ingredients being cayenne pepper, szechuan pepper, sesame seeds, hemp seeds, poppy seeds, roasted seaweed and dried orange peel. *Shichimi* is a common table spice mixture for sprinkling over many Japanese dishes. Available where Japanese food is sold.

Shio: In Japanese, *shio* refers to salt, and this is a salty Japanese sauce used for dipping yakitori before and after grilling.

Sumac: A dark, wine-colored spice with a sour taste, made from dried, ground-up sumac berries. *Sumac* is popular throughout the Middle East and is sprinkled over cooked kebabs, meat and fish as well as over breads and salads.

Tabil: A spice blend from Tunisia, consisting of caraway seeds, coriander seeds, hot red pepper flakes and garlic pounded in a mortar and then dried in the sun. It is used as a seasoning for meat, poultry and vegetable dishes.

Tandir: A traditional Azerbaijani flatbread cooked in a clay oven. The term *tandir* is also used in Turkey, Uzbekistan and other Central Asian republics to describe the clay oven used to bake different types of bread.

Taratoor: A popular Lebanese sesame sauce served with kebabs, fish and fried vegetables. It is made from sesame paste (tahini), lemon juice, garlic, cumin and salt and is available in stores selling Mediterranean or Middle Eastern foods.

Tzatziki: A traditional Greek dip made of yogurt and cucumber, seasoned with garlic, mint or dill, vinegar and olive oil. It is a standard accompaniment for Greek souvlaki or gyros (recipe page 222).

Ziran: This is a Xinjiang seasoning mostly used by Uighur Muslims in China to season their lamb kebabs. It consists of a mixture of powdered roasted cumin seeds, anise seeds, sesame seeds, salt and red pepper flakes.

INDEX